Happy HOLIDAYS

Thomas Murosky
Tyler Gayan

Published by Our Walk in Christ Publishing
State College, PA
www.owicpub.com

Happy Hellidays: When Holidays Lose Their Holiness

First Printing 2019
ISBN: 978-1-7325696-6-9 (sc)
ISBN: 978-1-7325696-7-6 (e)

The Internet addresses in this book are accurate at the time of publication. They are provided as a resource, but due to the nature of the Internet, those addresses may change.

Commitment to Open Source: Our Walk in Christ Publishing uses FOSS software where available. This book was produced with LibreOffice, GNU Image Manipulator Program, Sigil, Calibre, Blender, and the following open fonts: Abhaya Libre, Aftta Sans, Afta Serif, and Cookie. Chapter dividers obtained from https://publicdomainvectors.org. Audiobook edition produced with Audacity and Kid3.

LCCN: 2019942864

# Dedication

We are commanded by Scripture to be separate from the world, a peculiar people, called out to reach the world for Christ rather than succumbing to its ways.

We dedicate this book to the Universal Church as we appeal to them to return to the real roots of the holiday seasons and implore them to cast off consumerism and instead focus on God.

# Acknowledgments

Tyler wishes to acknowledge his family for raising him in the church. He has not only seen a unique side of this equation, but being raised in such an environment gives way to noticing important details and patterns that take place.

To this end, Tom wishes to acknowledge his family for the also unique experience of being raised outside the church. This, combined with becoming a Christian as an adult has helped him to see the difference between living by the Bible and living by following Leaders of the church. There is at times a difference.

Tom also wants to acknowledge his Aunt Char, Uncle Ron, and Cousin Ryan for the times their house was available for holidays when his home was not, and to his mom, Barb, for working so hard to provide all the needs in the house, even if it meant a little sacrifice.

For the technical aspects of the book, Tyler wishes to acknowledge Tom for the outlines, direction, and business end of writing this book. If it were not for his constant goading for essays, I would probably not have completed my portions of this book.

Tom thanks Tyler for the input and different writing styles and perspectives that can only be provided by younger eyes who are also dedicated to following Jesus obediently.

We both want to thank the beta readers for their input and quick edits and also a hefty shout out to Kate for doing the bulk of the editing.

# Contents

Dedication.................................................................3

Acknowledgments......................................................4

Introduction.............................................................7

What's In a Holy Day?..............................................13

The Baals of Today..................................................29

New Year Revolutions..............................................45

Buy My Valentine.....................................................63

A Pinch for Not Drinking Green................................81

The Bunny and the Tomb.........................................97

Happy Helloween...................................................113

Gobbled Up by Consumerism..................................131

Here Comes Satan Clause.......................................147

Old Testament Holidays..........................................169

General Bibliography..............................................180

Scripture Index.....................................................181

About the Authors.................................................183

Other Books by Thomas Murosky.............................184

# Introduction

## Happy Holidays!

### GROWING UP IN THE CHURCH

*H*olidays aren't a new concept, though they have morphed throughout the centuries of humanity's existence, but since before written history, people have called certain days special. I (Tyler) grew up in a church going family where holidays were very important to both our congregation and our home. We would garner fond memories during the Christmas eve service as I anxiously held the candle trying not to drop it; I had a very 'traditional' upbringing I would come to feel ambivalent about, trying to parse out the good values with cultural norms that wouldn't distinguish us as Christians.

I spent most of my holidays inside the church and having heard the same sermon every year, I don't know how it affects our attitude about holidays. The general consensus among common folk is Christians hold a more holy view of the celebrations, but looking back we seemed to segregate the church and family sections definitively and straight, often forgetting about the message 10 minutes later. There's only so much you can do to make a sermon seem fresh when it's tradition is over 20 centuries old and people don't find any new thing to grapple onto. The message departs the conscience of the congregation and becomes obscure. Another thing we have to consider is the lack of care by families to input these sermon's core points into their home during the various holiday seasons.

The culture, over hundreds of years, has had interesting interplay with the church, starting with a love of corporate worship, fading into neutrality, finally culminating with a final disdain, a mere rote observance. The middle ages is when the neutrality began. Roman Catholics led a compulsory service during those times. It was very rigid and punctual and the church resorted to punishment if their parsons failed to attend. This was a breeding ground for abuse and due to the pressure, I believe the masses developed a separate mind for the church, secluding a secular escape to contrast the compulsory attendance.

Though we are not directly punished for failing to attend holiday church services, a norm in most of the United States is to go to church with regular inquiries for failing to attend. We have similar problems today in regards to separate church minds and the holiday/secular split. *"A wall of separation of church and state"* was penned by the atheist president Thomas Jefferson to the Danbury Baptist Association in 1802 after they asked about being marginalized in society. Jefferson's meaning has since been grossly changed but it's original intent was to say *don't impose any religion on anyone*.

Let's go back to my 'traditional' upbringing while considering all these points and the schism of the church. My tradition was always going to a church service of some kind; a good 'ol American boy and family who never skipped. One thing I'm not grateful for is a then unforeseen side affect of the church and secular minds being so vastly different. Growing up as a member of a local congregation taught me from an early age that church is so important and deserves a different kind of attention, this messed with the six year old me. Christmas, Thanksgiving, and Easter sermons required a unique approach, one unique for church and not anywhere else. I think this is what brought me to a secular celebration.

## GROWING UP OUTSIDE THE CHURCH

Those who have known me (Tom) over the years know I am not generally a fan of holidays. Coming from a dysfunctional family and growing up outside the church, the holidays usually meant empty satisfaction in stuff and fake smiles by people who were supposed to love me, though at times it was hard to tell.

My first experience in a church service was an Easter holiday when I was still quite young, just about six years old. A few weeks prior to Easter in the mid 1980's we moved from the west coast into a house with my aunt, uncle, and cousin in a tiny town in Pennsylvania where the cows outnumbered the people three to one. My aunt and uncle at the time were the typical non-Christian of the mid 1980's, meaning they went to the service on Christmas and Easter because it was culturally expected. I was standing there with my mother humming along to these religious songs I did not understand when I asked who God is. She basically said she did not know and not to ask again. That was my only experience in church services as a kid and likewise my holidays were devoid of God, but filled with the culture.

All modern holidays, of course, are about stuff. What do you want for Christmas? What are you dressing as for Halloween? Are you watching the Macy's Day Parade? What about the football game? These are the questions asked of nearly everyone during the various holiday seasons, and as we celebrate holidays every few months, it seems the purpose is just to keep consumerism going.

Holidays used to be more about the important things. Christian families usually realize many holidays had connections to worship God, and they worshiped well. The non-Christians like myself often spent time together as families. Of course, the modern erosion of both faith and family lead both groups of people to the same conclusion: holidays are a time to buy gifts and to be pressured into the cultural and social norms of celebrating holidays at home, at work, at school, and everywhere.

Tracing the origin of holidays is a difficult task as most of them are shrouded in mystery and legend. Others have decried nearly every holiday as a Christianized celebration of old pagan holidays, and that may not be far from the truth. Philip Schaff wrote that Pope Gregory:

> Favored the Christianizing of heathen forms of cultus and popular festivals, and thereby contributed unconsciously to the paganizing of Christianity in the Middle Age. The calendar saints took the place of the ancient deities and Rome became a second time a pantheon. Against this new heathenism, with its sweeping abuses, pure Christianity was obliged with all earnestness and emphasis to protest[i].

Trying to push Christians to worship on days set apart for pagan worship of old is not a lot different than our modern interpretation of holidays. While the true origins of most holidays remains a mystery, it is clear the common root of modern holidays all trace back to corporate board rooms deciding what to market as seasonal trinkets this year. Rather than focusing on the consumer aspects or denouncing all holidays outright, we wanted to set out to do for holidays what God has done for us: Redeem them.

This book is about asking what holidays are, what they mean for our modern world, and how do we recapture what is important in each season. We want to revive the true meaning of holidays and call people to return to God, family, and faith. God, as we learn the point of holidays originally was to worship God, set aside work, and have faith that He will provide. Family, as we realize the nuclear

---

[i] History of the Christian Church Volume 3, Section 76

family, even though under assault, is still the greatest institution for raising our kids in love and truth. Faith, as we recognize the importance of having a strong root in spiritual understanding that gives us a focus on eternity rather than a focus on temporal things.

Join us as we explore the purpose and origin of the religious holidays in America. We will consider the roots, current practice, and what we should do as Christians moving forward. We will only be considering the holidays rooted in faith. We include Thanksgiving even though it is not a worldwide religious holiday because of its roots and purpose as they related to Christian practice in America.

# What's In a Holy Day?

The real meaning of the word 'holiday' is 'Holy Day'. In the broadest definition, Holy means 'set apart'. Thus, a holiday is a day set apart from other days for remembrance. Every settled culture had special days holy to their people, often coinciding with spring and autumn, as the times to sow and reap the harvest respectively. This was the case with the druids in Ireland whom Saint Patrick specifically engaged. Other holy days were celebrated around equinoxes corresponding to the longest and shortest days of the year. Still others celebrated the rising and setting of certain Zodiac constellations, giving rise to astrology and related arts. It is certain when God issued specific dates for the Israelites to set aside for rest and sacrifice, they were not the first culture to institute holidays, nor would they be the last.

## HOLIDAYS IN THE BIBLE

In the NASB Bible from which we will take most of our references, the specific word 'Holiday' only appears in the book of Ester. Many versions will even translate the first reference to holiday as merely 'a day to not pay taxes'. Even though the word does not make an appearance other places, the concept of a feast, celebration, and festival all carry the same meaning as 'holiday' in the Bible. The Israelites were not only offered many holidays, but they were even specifically commanded to celebrate several holy days throughout the year.

A festival was marked by several traits. Single-day festivals meant laborious work was forbidden, but preparations were allowed. For the festivals spanning several days, the first and the last day fell on a Sabbath or the people were otherwise forbidden to perform laborious work. Observing a Sabbath carries with it several benefits to our life. First, it prevents us from always being so focused on the results of our work. By letting a day go where we are not focused on results, we place some trust in God that He will provide even when we are not actively working. Next, it gives rest to our body and soul. When left to our own devices many people focus too much on work, but we often fail to notice rest will relax us and sharpen our body and mind for the following day. Also, while commanded to not work for the day we can focus on what is most important: faith and family. For this reason, festivals were often a time to sacrifice and to renew commitments to God, and to confess our frailty to Him. But family was also on the forefront of festivals. With the day's work forbidden, families worshiped together and with their communities.

Festivals also include the sharing of food. Often times we fail to realize sacrifice did not burn up the whole animal, but some of the beast went to the priests and the Levites leaving the rest of the sacrificed animal to be consumed by the person offering the sacrifice. As such, an abundance of food was available in the land during the feasts and those whom had more would share with those people not as materially blessed. The festivals were a time of community fellowship and sharing in the Old Testament law for the Israelites.

The sacrifice itself was the most important part of the festivals. The command for various holidays in Israel was to offer up the first fruits, the portion of the harvest, a sin offering, or some other very specific sacrifice. As already mentioned, often times portions of the sacrifice were consumed by the person offering the sacrifice.

Finally, the festivals were a communal fellowship. People who had more gave to those with less. Shared items usually constituted food, but could include toys for the children, articles of clothing, or tools. We also know several of the festivals required traveling to Jerusalem, the place God chose for His name to dwell, and community would arrive in large traveling groups such as those whom Jesus traveled with when He was a boy (*Luke 2:41-45*).

## JEWISH HOLIDAYS

God gave the Israelites specific feasts to celebrate or else be cut off from the community. These feasts mandated specific days of rest and sacrifices. The most important of these was the Feast of Unleavened Bread, during which the Passover was remembered. The other two major feasts were the start of the growing season (Feast of Harvest or Feast of Weeks) and the harvest time (Feast of the Ingathering).

The three prescribed feasts were to be celebrated by all people in the nation, and the celebration was to occur at a specific place. During the writing of the law, Moses recorded the celebration was to be held at *the place where the LORD your God chooses to establish His name (Deuteronomy 16:6)*. *2 Chronicles 6:5-6* identifies that location as Jerusalem. *Deuteronomy 16:16-17* commands all males were to make a pilgrimage to Jerusalem three times a year. By extension from other scriptures, the family also traveled with the men who presented offerings for themselves and their families. So among the feasts prescribed throughout the year, three of them required a pilgrimage and a significant sacrifice.

In addition to the three required feasts, there were some other annual festivities the Jewish nation included on their calendar, some coming directly from God, but a few coming from other traditions. We have explained in detail the feasts in the Appendix of this book and included a table summarizing them here.

## FEASTS IN THE KINGLY HISTORICAL RECORD

Moses left the Israelite army in the capable hands of Joshua who reiterated the importance of following God, but after Joshua died the people all but forgot their God who freed them from Egypt. Moses delivered promises for following God in *Deuteronomy 28*, but the fourteen verses of blessings were overshadowed with fifty-four verses of curses for disobedience. Near the end of the Canaanite conquest, the people were already forgetting about the Law and were rebuked by God (*Judges 2:1-5*). But after Joshua died the people turned to the pagan gods around them (*Judges 2:11-16*), setting up several cycles of obedience and disobedience characteristic of the days of the judges. During these times without a direct leader, they did not follow the mandates of the law. It was during these days the people would rebel against God and then find themselves oppressed by the very nations He commanded them to destroy. He would then raise up judges who would guide the people back to the Law of God (*Judges 2:16-23*).

The people finally asked for a king when Samuel, the final judge, was growing old because his sons did not walk in his ways. Of course, God knew the people would eventually ask for a king and Moses gave some specific instructions for the ruler to follow in *Deuteronomy 17:14-20*:

| Holiday | Biblical Context | Jewish Date | Modern Date |
|---------|------------------|-------------|-------------|
| Feast of Passover | Exodus 12:1-4, Matthew 26:17-20 | Day 14 of Nisan | March or April |

Each household would take one lamb each for themselves according to their father's house. In the case that a neighbor didn't have a big enough house, they would share a lamb with their neighbor according to the number of combined people under the roof.

| Holiday | Biblical Context | Jewish Date | Modern Date |
|---------|------------------|-------------|-------------|
| Feast of Unleavened Bead | Exodus 12:15-20 | Days 15-21 of Nisan | March or April |

For one week, the Israelites eat unleavened bread; whoever does not will be banished from the nation. The first and last day of the week is a sabbath.

| Holiday | Biblical Context | Jewish Date | Modern Date |
|---------|------------------|-------------|-------------|
| Feast of the First Fruits | Leviticus 23:9-14 | Day 16 of Nisan or Day 6 of Sivan | March or April |

The Israelites would take a sheaf of fruits and give it to the priest, one day after the sabbath, the priest would wave it in front of the Lord. At that same time, the Israelites would offer a unblemished one year old male lamb as a burnt offering, two tenths offering of ephah mixed with oil and fine flour, they would burn that as a pleasing aroma, and a fourth of a hin of wine. You shouldn't eat bread, roasted grain,or new growth until sacrifices are made and this should be done within 7 complete Sabbaths.

| Holiday | Biblical Context | Jewish Date | Modern Date |
|---------|------------------|-------------|-------------|
| Feast of Pentecost (Hharvest of weeks) | Deuteronomy 26:9-12, Acts 2:1 | Day 6 of Sivan (50 days after Barley Harvest | May or June |

After giving tithes to the Lord, the more fortunate give to the less fortunate regardless of anything.

| Holiday | Biblical Context | Jewish Date | Modern Date |
|---------|------------------|-------------|-------------|
| Feast of Trumpets (Rosh Hashanah) | Numbers 29:1-6 | Day 1 & 2 of Tishri | September or October |

The Israelites should have a convocation and shouldn't do any work. Offer burnt offering of smooth aroma to God, also offer one bull, one ram, and 7 male lambs without defect that's one year old. For their grain offering, they should bring a fine flour mix with oil; 3/10 of an ephah for the bull, 2/10 for the ram, and 1/10 for each of the lambs. Offer one male goat for a sin offering for you.

| Holiday | Biblical Context | Jewish Date | Modern Date |
|---------|------------------|-------------|-------------|
| Day of Atonement (Yom Kippur) | Leviticus 23:26-32, Hebrews 9:7 | Day 10 of Tishri | September or October |

The Israelites would have a convocation for this day and present a fire offering to the Lord. There is no work on this day, the consequence for not humbling yourself on this day is being exiled from your people, likewise with the work, but the consequence will be death.

| Holiday | Biblical Context | Jewish Date | Modern Date |
|---------|------------------|-------------|-------------|
| Feast of Booths, Tabernacle, or Ingathering | Leviticus 23:33-43, John 7:2 | Days 15-21 of Tishri | September or October |

The Israelites would have a convocation. No customary work* on this day, however, the celebration would involve gathering palm tree bushels and worshiping the Lord for seven days. For this period of time, the people would live in booths as a reminder of how God brought them out of Egypt.

| Holiday | Biblical Context | Jewish Date | Modern Date |
|---------|------------------|-------------|-------------|
| Feast of Purim (Lots) | Esther 9:18-32 | Day 14 and 15 of Adar | February or March |

The Jewish people would feast and hand out presents to one another, everyone would help out the poor, and God would let them rest from their enemies.

> *When you enter the land which the LORD your God gives you, and you possess it and live in it, and you say, 'I will set a king over me like all the nations who are around me,' you shall surely set a king over you whom the LORD your God chooses, one from among your countrymen you shall set as king over yourselves; you may not put a foreigner over yourselves who is not your countryman. Moreover, he shall not multiply horses for himself, nor shall he cause the people to return to Egypt to multiply horses, since the LORD has said to you, 'You shall never again return that way.' He shall not multiply wives for himself, or else his heart will turn away; nor shall he greatly increase silver and gold for himself.*

> *Now it shall come about when he sits on the throne of his kingdom, he shall write for himself a copy of this law on a scroll in the presence of the Levitical priests. It shall be with him and he shall read it all the days of his life, that he may learn to fear the LORD his God, by carefully observing all the words of this law and these statutes, that his heart may not be lifted up above his countrymen and that he may not turn aside from the commandment, to the right or the left, so that he and his sons may continue long in his kingdom in the midst of Israel.*

From these verses, we see the Mosaic Law set a few requirements for the office of the king. First, he was not to build up a large army. This was so the king would not become prideful in his army, turning his trust onto himself rather than to God. David violated this command as recorded in *2 Samuel 24*.

Another requirement was the king was to write his own copy of the law in the presence of the priests and to use that copy of the law, in his own hand, as a daily record of how to rule the kingdom. This was to prevent the king from thinking himself above the rest of the people. We do not have a record of any king who actually fulfilled the command to write his own copy of the law.

Samuel placed a king over the people as they requested but the kingship seemed to mark the beginning of the end of the celebration of the feasts. We know Saul celebrated a New Moon festival (*1 Samuel 20:5*), so it is possible he still commanded the other feasts in the law. We do not have a specific record of the required feasts during David's reign, but we do see David commanding Solomon to observe the laws laid down by Moses, which included the feasts (*1 Kings 2:1-4*). There is a record of Solomon commanding the Levites regarding the duties of their appointed service including obeying the commandments for the required festivals (*1 Chronicles 23:31*). Shortly after this period when Solomon turned from God the commands of Moses and the law delivered on Mount Sinai were all but forgotten.

The Israelites split into two kingdoms after Solomon's reign and part of the fragmented kingdom plummeted into the depths of sin. They experienced the various curses pronounced by God and suffered famines, wars, defeat, and droughts. A few kings were recorded as following the ways of God, most notably Hezekiah. After a long line of unfaithful kings, Hezekiah cleaned the temple of idolatry (*2 Chronicles 29:3-11*) and commanded the people to celebrate the Passover for the first time since the days of Solomon (*2 Chronicles 30:1-9*). The days for the Israelite people[i] to worship God came to a close when Hezekiah's son, Manasseh, became king. He reigned for 55 years and rebuilt the pagan worship his father had destroyed.

Josiah was the great grandson of Hezekiah and a faithful king who once again brought Israel back to God. While purging the temple of the vile idols, the priest Hilkiah found a copy of the Law of God (*2 Kings 22:8*). This book was likely not seen for decades. It was probably brought back into the temple by Hezekiah and left untouched during the pagan times of Manasseh and Amon. The book was read to Josiah and he realized just how far Israel had fallen (*2 Kings*

---

[i] Here we are using Israelite to mean the religious origin of people, not the divided kingdoms of Israel and Judah.

*22:11-13*). God's judgment was set, but God delayed wrath because of Josiah's faithfulness. The righteous king restored the Passover feast and the people celebrated for a week (*2 Chronicles 35:16-19*).

The final kings in Jerusalem were also wicked and God saw fit to remove the Israelites from their country for a period of exile. Prior to the exile, Jeremiah prophesied about the destruction of Judah:

> Therefore thus says the LORD of hosts, 'Because you have not obeyed My words, behold, I will send and take all the families of the north,' declares the LORD, 'and I will send to Nebuchadnezzar king of Babylon, My servant, and will bring them against this land and against its inhabitants and against all these nations round about; and I will utterly destroy them and make them a horror and a hissing, and an everlasting desolation. Moreover, I will take from them the voice of joy and the voice of gladness, the voice of the bridegroom and the voice of the bride, the sound of the millstones and the light of the lamp. This whole land will be a desolation and a horror, and these nations will serve the king of Babylon seventy years (*Jeremiah 25:8-11*).

Just as Jeremiah prophesied, the king of Babylon conquered the land and carried the people into exile (*2 Chronicles 36:15-20*). The time of the exile: 70 years corresponding to the 70 Sabbath years the Israelites refused to honor (*2 Chronicles 36:21*). We see here a direct connection between the failure to keep the required feasts and the Israelite conquest at the hands of Assyria and Babylon. May we learn from this and seek to honor God in our own life!

During the reign of Cyrus, the Israelites were allowed to return to their homeland, but even that was a fulfillment of the prophecies of the men of God. *Ezra 1:1* tells us the proclamation was to fulfill the words of *Jeremiah 29:10*:

> For thus says the LORD, 'When seventy years have been completed for Babylon, I will visit you and fulfill My good word to you, to bring you back to this place.'

The Israelites knew they were exiled into Assyria and Babylon because they were unfaithful to the commands, which included the feasts and holidays. The restoration of the kingdom in the time of Ezra saw a full revival back to the commandments of the Mosaic Law. Both Ezra and Nehemiah record the sacrifices were carried out by the priests under the specific instructions and the people resumed celebrating the feasts:

> They celebrated the Feast of Booths, as it is written, and offered the fixed number of burnt offerings daily, according to the ordinance, as each day required (Ezra 3:4).

> They found written in the law how the LORD had commanded through Moses that the sons of Israel should live in booths during the feast of the seventh month (Nehemiah 8:14).

This marked the beginning of the return to faithfulness to following the commands. However, it also created the sect of Pharisees who focused more on following regulations and forgetting the heart behind the feasts. This point is very significant because it is the same with us today. The calendar rolls around to Easter, Christmas, Halloween, and so on. We forget about the significance of the holidays to God, and focus on our own pleasures. Like the Israelites before the exile, we have forgotten to worship God, but like the Pharisees afterward, we keep the letter of the law (or in modern times, the cultural pressure to engage), but our hearts are far from the God who makes holidays matter.

## Holy Days in the New Testament

The coming of Jesus did not totally cancel out all of the Jewish feasts. Even throughout his life, He was obedient to the feasts. As a twelve year old, Jesus went to Jerusalem with His parents in obedience to the law (Luke 2:41-43). During His earthly ministry Jesus returned for the annual feasts (John

*2:13*). The verses following demonstrate to us that Jesus did not just go up out of obligation, but rather for zeal:

> *And He found in the temple those who were selling oxen and sheep and doves, and the money changers seated at their tables. And He made a scourge of cords, and drove them all out of the temple, with the sheep and the oxen; and He poured out the coins of the money changers and overturned their tables; and to those who were selling the doves He said, "Take these things away; stop making My Father's house a place of business (John 2:14-16)."*

Jesus obeyed out of love for God, arrived in Jerusalem during other feasts (*John 5:1*) and even taught in the synagogue at another (*John 7:14*). Of even greater significance was His final sacrifice. Jesus partook of the Passover meal, and then He became the Passover lamb, He was unbroken, without blemish, sacrificed for the sins of His people.

The Christian connection to the Jewish feasts does not end with Christ's last breath, but even His resurrection was on the third day indicating He rested on the Sabbath before rising. But after He made himself known to the disciples, they were to wait in Jerusalem until the Holy Spirit was given to them (*Acts 1:4-5*). That occurred on no other day than Pentecost, making yet another connection to the Old Testament feasts.

We do not have any specific commands to celebrate the Jewish feasts, but they do not completely disappear from the early founding of the church. In *Acts 12:1-2*, James was martyred by Herod and Peter was arrested, mostly as a means to please the Jews; these occurred during the Feast of Unleavened Bread. We can gather from context Herod was trying to please the Jews, and that probably means the early church was not keeping the feasts as prescribed. We can also infer they were not keeping the feasts based on the Council at Jerusalem. The council met to discuss Jewish customs among the Gentiles, primarily being the circumcision, but by inferences the rest of the Jewish ceremonial customs. They come to this conclusion:

*For it seemed good to the Holy Spirit and to us to lay upon you no greater burden than these essentials: that you abstain from things sacrificed to idols and from blood and from things strangled and from fornication; if you keep yourselves free from such things, you will do well. Farewell (Acts 15:28-29).*

This was expanded upon in the New Testament which had not yet been written, but the feasts, being part of the Jewish ceremonies, were not specifically commanded to be observed for believers.

This being said, there was also not a specific command to not celebrate the feasts. It is clear Paul still held to many customs as a means of respect for such an audience:

*To the Jews I became as a Jew, so that I might win Jews; to those who are under the Law, as under the Law though not being myself under the Law, so that I might win those who are under the Law (1 Corinthians 9:20).*

He also proclaims that a person keeping the feasts to honor God in some way is also in the right under his conscience (*Romans 14:5-6*). This section on conscience identifies that some people will hold to some rituals in their life for whatever reason: family upbringing, cultural festivities, or practical habit. Paul does not condemn such a celebration, so long as it does not interfere with practical worship of God (*Colossians 2:16-17*).

To contrast this, he was concerned about the legalistic celebration of the feasts where people thought it would make them right with God:

*However at that time, when you did not know God, you were slaves to those which by nature are no gods. But now that you have come to know God, or rather to be known by God, how is it that you turn back again to the weak and worthless elemental things, to which you desire to be enslaved all over again? You observe days and months and seasons and years (Galatians 4:8-10).*

So keeping a festival as part of heritage or culture is not to be condemned so long as you do not believe participation will make you right with God. Likewise, we are not to argue with people who participate in such a festival except where professing Christians believe the observance of the ceremony makes them right with Christ.

## THE NEW SACRAMENT

The connection to the feasts in the New Testament church lay in the institution of the Lord's Supper, or Communion, which Jesus pronounces during the Passover:

*While they were eating, He took some bread, and after a blessing He broke it, and gave it to them, and said, "Take it; this is My body."And when He had taken a cup and given thanks, He gave it to them, and they all drank from it. And He said to them, "This is My blood of the covenant, which is poured out for many. Truly I say to you, I will never again drink of the fruit of the vine until that day when I drink it new in the kingdom of God (Mark 14:22-25)."*

Paul identifies the doctrine regarding Communion in *1 Corinthians*. The key point is the differences between the Jewish festival and Communion in the heart of the partaker. We are not to approach the table out of obligation or law, but out of sincerity in our repentance (*1 Corinthians 5:8*). Paul explains this requirement of repentance further:

*Therefore whoever eats the bread or drinks the cup of the Lord in an unworthy manner, shall be guilty of the body and the blood of the Lord. But a man must examine himself, and in so doing he is to eat of the bread and drink of the cup. For he who eats and drinks, eats and drinks judgment to himself if he does not judge the body rightly (1 Corinthians 11:27-29).*

So the only connection we have now is to partake in the Lord's Table with personal self-examination, not out of regulation, but out of true repentance when we have accepted the sacrifice of Jesus. Any celebration beyond this is not a requirement of the Scriptures, but neither is participation condemned. Of course, we are assuming at this point our readers are Christians. If not, please read the following Gospel and ask if you are a sinner in need of salvation.

## THE GOSPEL

We are sinners: inherently, immutably, and unstoppably. That is the ultimate problem with our human condition. We can't get into heaven but instead are destined for its under earth alternative. If you want to go to hell, then these next 500 words will be absolutely useless to you, but if you are interested in going to heaven, keep reading to find out the only way to find a true relationship with God.

First things first, we are sinners, and without the help of a special someone, will remain so forever; only when we embrace ourselves as sinners can we move onto the solution. The Bible makes it abundantly clear via *Romans 3:10-18* we are perpetual evil doers. It is our connection to Adam that gives us birth-laden inclinations to sin (*Romans 5:12*). We are presently born in post-crucifixion and post-resurrection times, meaning we live when Christ already rose from the tomb proving death can be defeated for us if we use the power of Jesus Christ:

*If you confess with your mouth Jesus as Lord, and believe in your heart that God raised Him from the dead, you will be saved (Romans 10:9).*

Once we accept God as our savior, we should start to feel a hankering to read the Bible:

*As a deer pants for the water brooks, So my soul pants for You, O God (Psalm 42:1).*

Even if you don't desire to read the Scriptures, it's a good practice that only yields good results. Reading the Bible is vital for growing in faith (*2 Timothy 3:16*) and it is necessary for growing closer to God and retracting farther from sin. Along the same lines, memorizing scriptures is useful when training ourselves to avoid sin. God always provides a path out of temptation (*1 Corinthians 10:13*). Praying and talking to God never hurts, and it helps develop our relationship with Him. Finally, finding a wiser Christian to teach us is probably the best thing for a young Christian to help understand and apply the Scriptures. This could be a mentoring relationship (most preferred) but also could be reading great books by sound Bible scholars.

A lot of people will advise new believers to join a "Bible believing church" just after starting their journey with God. That's well and good, but what is such a church? Nearly every church will profess to be "Bible believing", but many of those do not take the Scriptures seriously. Some churches abuse their authority, teaching their flock of church goers in wrong ways. Some churches go to unruly lengths of extremes leading their congregations away from God. A Bible believing church would be one that addresses all aspects of the Word not excluding some teachings or adding others.

We suggest an incubation period to grow in your new found faith before committing to attending regular services. The goal is to find a good church, but you should know the basic truths of Scripture before committing yourself to a congregation. Our pastors and churches are supposed to be equipping us with knowledge of the faith (*Ephesians 4:11-12*), and it is best to know what that means. Once, however, you have studied your scriptures and learned from a mentor, it is time to search for a local congregation which is committed to the things of God.

## WHERE DID THESE HOLIDAYS COME FROM?

Now that we have studied the Scriptures as it relates to holidays and festivals, it begs a fascinating question: where did these holidays all come from if not from the Bible? The problem we find is there is not one time, point, or even fully agreed upon history for our Christian holidays. To that end, we will explore the most popular traditions and beliefs where the popular Christian holidays have come from, and more importantly what they have evolved into. We will conclude each chapter with a call to return to what a holiday should be, discuss whether we should celebrate holidays, and what our Christian conduct surrounding those holidays should be.

# The Baals of Today

God takes His law seriously, and though He has not directly addressed the consumer culture of the west, the Scriptures offer plenty of advice about how we should interact with the societies in which we find ourselves residing. In this chapter we examine the commands regarding covetousness, contentment, and even learn the Devil's occupation (at least according to us). Let us examine in detail the Baals of today's world.

## YOU SHALL NOT COVET

Attached to the Ten Commandments (*Exodus 20:1-17*) is the final proclamation regarding covetousness:

*You shall not covet your neighbor's house; you shall not covet your neighbor's wife or his male servant or his female servant or his ox or his donkey or anything else that belongs to your neighbor (verse 17).*

Covetousness at its core means desire, specifically such desire leading to temptation to break a variety of God's moral laws. Covetousness is to see something we want and seek an occasion of illegitimately gaining it. Coveting is not seeing a nice watch, desiring to get one like it, and working toward the goal, saving up to buy it. Notice the specific command is in regard to your neighbor's wife, or servant, or animal. This means we must not flirt with our neighbor's wife in the hopes to separate her from her husband unto your own service. Same with the animals. It was not wrong to desire another ox to plow the fields, but to steal our neighbor's ox was to act on covetous desires, and that is what God condemns. Likewise in our modern world, we ought to live moderately and not let "the Jones's" new car inflame us to upgrade our own perfectly functioning vehicle.

God knows the emotions which could easily follow covetousness: greed, envy, and even theft or murder. In His command regarding the people, He was safeguarding them against these sins, though many violations were displayed in scripture because the people did not heed His warning. Not long after Moses died the people were destroying Jericho under Joshua's leadership. The command was easy enough: Destroy everything (*Joshua 6:17-18*)! But one man, Achan, was unfaithful. He saw gold, silver, and a coat and took them, obeying his covetous thoughts over the command from God. *Joshua 7:21* records in his confession: he coveted the items devoted to destruction and took them instead for himself thinking he could hide his actions from God. Had he just wanted them without succumbing to temptation, all would have been well, but following through his act of covetousness led to his death by stoning.

David also succumbed to covetousness as he was walking along the palace roof one night. He looked down and saw a beautiful woman bathing and coveted her. He inquired of his servants who she was, and the answer came back: she was another man's wife. This was not just some random man, however, David would have known Uriah because he was actually one of David's thirty-seven mighty men (*2 Samuel 23:39*)! He had the opportunity to come to his senses, but instead he sent word through his servants to bring her up to him, and as king, she could not refuse. They

committed adultery, got pregnant, and then David killed
Uriah by sending him to the front of the battle. These sins
became not only a stain on David's character, but also the
beginning of the downfall of his very dynasty. All this
because David coveted a woman who was not his (*2 Samuel
11:2-5*).

The New Testament also records an incident worthy of
discussion. Simon was a Samaritan sorcerer, probably not
unlike many religious charlatans of today. He used his
religion to gain money (*Acts 8:9-13*). When it was reported to
the Apostles the Samaritans were being baptized they sent
Peter and John to pray for the people and instruct them in
the Lord. Simon was among those whom Philip had baptized
but when he saw the Holy Spirit descending on people at the
mere touch from Peter and John, he showed his true heart
when he offered the Apostles money to give him the same
power (*Acts 8:14-19*). Peter saw right through Simon
admonishing him to repent, for coveting the power of the
Apostles was not trusting God in faith.

The Lord knew what He was doing when he added the
commandments against coveting into the Ten Commandments. Wickedness is bound up with covetousness
whether it be desiring power, wealth, or sexual gratification.
God has declared how He will handle those who live a
covetous life:

> *Woe to those who scheme iniquity,*
> *Who work out evil on their beds!*
> *When morning comes, they do it,*
> *For it is in the power of their hands.*
> *They covet fields and then seize them,*
> *And houses, and take them away.*
> *They rob a man and his house,*
> *A man and his inheritance.*
>
> *Therefore thus says the Lord,*

> *"Behold, I am planning against this family a calamity*
> *From which you cannot remove your necks;*
> *And you will not walk haughtily,*
> *For it will be an evil time.*
> *(Micah 2:1-3)*

Proverbs also warns that covetousness leads us to despair:

> *The desire of the sluggard puts him to death,*
> *For his hands refuse to work;*
> *All day long he is craving,*
> *While the righteous gives and does not hold back.*
> *Proverbs 21:25-26*

The problem with covetousness is for many people who get used to acquiring 'stuff', the desire is never full. We try to accumulate more and more hoping to find the one purchase truly making us happy, only to find that happiness is fleeting. We will discuss the folly of happiness later in this chapter on the section regarding the thrill of the purchase. For now, suffice it to say gaining material goods does not bring fulfillment, and Jesus Himself talked about such a person desiring wealth:

> *For what will it profit a man if he gains the world and forfeits his soul*
> *(Matthew 16:26)?*

Furthermore, the accumulation of possessions will not help to clarify who we are, rather it muddles our own understanding about ourselves.

## POLLUTED BY MARKETING

Many have speculated on the Devil's occupation in our modern world. Some Hollywood productions like *Devil's Advocate* suggest he is a lawyer because they are into everything. Truly, what business market is not in need of a good lawyer for settling disputes and writing contracts?

Others in the same establishment have said through the television program *Lucifer* that he would run a bar as they are a hub of sin in our culture. This could make sense in light of the sin so often accompanying the flow of alcohol. We suggest neither occupation clearly reflects what the Devil does in his daily work and that is part of his deception. Though sin is certainly present in both those environments, sin is present everywhere in our world, but the Devil is not just about practicing sin, but rather he wants to get other people to practice sin. Let's look at his Biblical début:

> Now the serpent was more crafty than any beast of the field which the LORD God had made. And he said to the woman, "Indeed, has God said, 'You shall not eat from any tree of the garden'?" The woman said to the serpent, "From the fruit of the trees of the garden we may eat; but from the fruit of the tree which is in the middle of the garden, God has said, 'You shall not eat from it or touch it, or you will die.'" The serpent said to the woman, "You surely will not die! For God knows that in the day you eat from it your eyes will be opened, and you will be like God, knowing good and evil." When the woman saw that the tree was good for food, and that it was a delight to the eyes, and that the tree was desirable to make one wise, she took from its fruit and ate; and she gave also to her husband with her, and he ate. Then the eyes of both of them were opened, and they knew that they were naked; and they sewed fig leaves together and made themselves loin coverings (Genesis 3:1-7).

We see from this scripture the Devil is crafty. That is to say he is smooth in speech, calculated, and speaks to induce behavior in his listeners. He started this dialog by getting Eve to question the only command God gave the two humans. He then gave her a different message informing her she would not die, but instead God was trying to restrict her, but he was trying to make her free. All this caused Eve to question God's word and do an act she otherwise would not have done. In short, the Devil marketed to Eve a different plan.

The Devil is a marketer, always probing and tempting to engage his subjects in behavior they may not otherwise do. Such is the case of marketers in our world. Their goal is not to inform us of their products, it is to convince us to buy their products. Modern day marketing approaches have demonstrated they will do absolutely everything to get a person to buy their goods whether it is in the subject's best interest or not. Thus, the Devil is employed in the marketing business.

Some would say the objective of marketing is to inform consumers of new products. We do not believe, however, this is a matter of education, but of subversion. If the purpose of commercials were exclusively to inform, we would have objective, fact-based commercials. But the reality is we see emotional appeals designed to make us discontented. Modern commercials teach us desire for their product as the solution to our woes...for now. They want us to covet the gizmos and gadgets we see so much we will spend every dollar we have in the pursuit of our own happiness or to avoid the social stigma of not having the latest car, phone, or smart device. Neil Postman wrote of commercials in *The Disappearance of Childhood*[1]:

> "The TV commercial does not present products in a form that calls upon analytical skills or what we customarily think of as rational and mature judgment. It is not facts that are offered to the consumer but idols, to which both adults and children can attach themselves with equal devotion and without the burden of logic or verification. It is, therefore, misleading even to call this form of communication "commercials," since they disdain the rhetoric of business and do their work largely with the symbols and rhetoric of religion."

Postman continues to describe commercials as modern day parables where the structure consists of sin, a solution, and a vision of heaven for those smart enough to follow the advice of the perfect informants of the proper way. Taken

---

[1] *The Disappearance of Childhood*, Neil Postman, 1994, Vintage Books

together with our topic on holidays, how could your children possibly have a good Easter or Christmas without new toys and gifts created in the image of popular television characters. It is sad that even cheap knock-off gifts are presented in buying bins designed to match the accepted colors of seasonal events.

Marketing seeks to breed covetousness, which is not enduring. The idea is to convince us our lives are not complete without their new solutions. Like a child anticipating Christmas morning, we flock to stores in droves at the release of a new iPhone or the latest video game franchise expansion giving more of our hard-earned money for the same thing we already have. But the feeling does not last. We have forgotten that in Him we live and breathe and have our being.

## THE THRILL OF THE PURCHASE

Consider again our child during the hours preceding Christmas. The evening of the holy grail of kid-dom is a long and painful night as he anticipates the overindulgence of new toys. Adults get those feelings when the prospect of a new phone, video game, movie, or other trinket seeks our attention. If we have the willpower to fight the feelings we risk going back to purchase the item in the next few days. We justify when we will pay for it, how we will pay for it, and our culture generally goes further into debt on credit cards or making payments to finance large purchases. We do this for the thrill of the purchase, believing that buying trinkets fills the hole in our heart and makes our life complete. This is folly.

> *He who loves pleasure will become a poor man;*
> *He who loves wine and oil will not become rich.*
> *Proverbs 21:17*

Not only will the misguided purchase of products fail to satisfy, but the money we spend on them will lead us wanting for more, failing to meet our retirement goals, and preventing us from helping our neighbors when times become tough. We become slaves to the marketers who seek to extract our funds. We become choked by the goods of the material world, and if we are not careful, we may become counted as those thrown among the thorns:

*Others were the ones on whom seed was sown among the thorns; these are the ones who have heard the word, but the worries of the world, and the deceitfulness of riches, and the desires for other things enter in and choke the word, and it becomes unfruitful (Mark 4:18-19).*

This is precisely what has been occurring in the western culture of late and the influence is both inside and outside the church. American Christians, in general, have allowed marketing to breed covetousness in our hearts, growing the desire to buy the latest gizmos and gadgets. We spend money that could go to other endeavors on streaming services, monthly payments, and empty stuff, all because we have bought into a cultural idea that having material goods means we are better people, and the belief that having pleasure will give us relaxation. We are being choked by the thorns and if the parable is true, we will become unfruitful... perhaps we have already withered.

We have to learn that wealth and material possessions are fleeting. They are not entirely bad, and like Paul, I (Tom) have lived in abundance and I have lived in poverty; both have their advantages and their pitfalls. Belongings are just things and we have no right to judge our neighbors hearts merely by his possessions, but the question remains ours to answer. Are we placing our trust in things? Are we placing our trust in wealth? Consider what Solomon wrote in *Ecclesiastes 5:10:*

*He who loves money will not be satisfied with money, nor he who loves abundance with its income. This too is vanity.*

We leave this section by clarifying we are not against material belongings. Our objection here is how marketing lends to covetousness and tries to tell us our life will be complete when we buy a product or service. The present American model of consumerism gives us idols to worship as people or products and distractions to keep us focused on the world rather than God. It seeks to takes all our money before we can decide how best to use the resources God entrusted to us for His ultimate glory. Truly the thrill of the sale will not last, and the purchase of fleeting merchandise captures those resources from going into Kingdom purposes.

## CONSUMERISM AND CONTENTMENT

We have already looked at a verse from Solomon about riches, but let us examine a few more verses in *Ecclesiastes 5*:

*There is a grievous evil which I have seen under the sun: riches being hoarded by their owner to his hurt. When those riches were lost through a bad investment and he had fathered a son, then there was nothing to support him. As he had come naked from his mother's womb, so will he return as he came. He will take nothing from the fruit of his labor that he can carry in his hand. This also is a grievous evil—exactly as a man is born, thus will he die. So what is the advantage to him who toils for the wind? (13-16)*

Consumerism directs us toward consumption, and like evil, consumption is never full. Solomon warns about hording money, because such hording tends to make us covetous. We will take nothing with us out of this world. Jesus illustrates the same principle in *Luke 12:16-21*:

*And He told them a parable, saying, "The land of a rich man was very productive. And he began reasoning to himself, saying, 'What shall I do, since I have no place to store my crops?' Then he said, 'This is what I will do: I will tear down my barns and build larger ones, and there I will store all my grain and my goods. And I will say to my soul, "Soul, you have many goods laid up for many years to come; take your ease, eat, drink and be merry."' But God said to him, 'You fool! This very night your soul is required of you; and now who will own what you have prepared?' So is the man who stores up treasure for himself, and is not rich toward God."*

Jesus was not saying money and wealth is bad, in fact the scripture uses many examples of wealth being used in positive ways and even calling it a blessing (*Luke 6:38*). The problem here is the storing up of wealth made this foolish man want to trust in his possessions as his security. It is easy for us to fall into the trap of trusting our wealth and acquisitions. Paul addressed the wealthy people in the church specifically in *1 Timothy 6:17-19*:

*Instruct those who are rich in this present world not to be conceited or to fix their hope on the uncertainty of riches, but on God, who richly supplies us with all things to enjoy. Instruct them to do good, to be rich in good works, to be generous and ready to share, storing up for themselves the treasure of a good foundation for the future, so that they may take hold of that which is life indeed.*

The rich were not commanded to give everything to the church, but to use their money to bless the community around them. The ultimate command is to not look to our money as our source of trust or decline, but that we would instead we dwell richly on the power of Christ no matter our financial situation. Paul says in *Philippians 4:8*:

*Finally, brethren, whatever is true, whatever is honorable, whatever is right, whatever is pure, whatever is lovely, whatever is of good repute, if there is any excellence and if anything worthy of praise, dwell on these things.*

Paul continues the next few verses talking about contentment in whatever situation he finds himself. If we have extra money, praise God that we have some. If we do not have extra money and times are tight, praise God for the power to fight another day. A content person can learn not to worry in the tough times and he does not dwell on his wealth during the times of abundance. Thus, we should all learn not to think of things as a means to our happiness.

The Rich Young Ruler (*Matthew 19:16-22*) seemed to trust in his possessions. He asks Jesus what he must do to inherit eternal life, which Christ first replied to obey the commands. The young man was clearly not content with the answer considering he believed he followed all of those commands from his youth. Like an affluent person who collects stuff, joy escapes this young man, and he still seeks more. Jesus tested him on the first command: sell your possessions and follow Him. The young man demonstrated very clearly he had truly not obeyed even the first of the commands, placing his possessions before his service to God.

God knows our things and affluence do not guide us to happiness, but in contrast, they often lead to our downfall. Moses's words recorded in Deuteronomy demonstrate just how well God knew his people, and about the future affluence in the land flowing with milk and honey. He had this to say:

> Beware that you do not forget the Lord your God by not keeping His commandments and His ordinances and His statutes which I am commanding you today; otherwise when you have eaten and are satisfied, and have built good houses and have lived in them, and when your herds and your flocks multiply, and all that you have multiplies, then your heart will become proud and you will forget the Lord your God who brought you out from the land of Egypt, out of the house of slavery (Deuteronomy 8:11-14).

We fail to become content when we start focusing on worldly things being thrown at us in marketing. To contrast this point, the Israelites were told to keep the commandments and ordinances passed down through Moses. In the New Testament we find general principles to help us focus on God over riches. The author of Hebrews says to be free from the love of money, contrasting that desire with contentment (*Hebrews 13:5*). Paul echoes the same sentiment in *Philippians 4:11-12*:

> Not that I speak from want, for I have learned to be content in whatever circumstance I am. I know how to get along with humble means, and I also know how to live in prosperity; in any and every circumstance I have learned the secret of being filled and going hungry, both of having abundance and suffering need.

Paul's disposition of heart was not dependent on his stuff and circumstances. We need to take this lesson from our heads into our hearts, learning things do not have the power to bring us joy, and that lacking material goods cannot bring us to sorrow. Riches are fleeting, and we are given so many warnings about wealth because of the ease by which money can be lost.

## THE BALANCE

> Keep deception and lies far from me,
> Give me neither poverty nor riches;
> Feed me with the food that is my portion,
> That I not be full and deny You and say,
> "Who is the Lord?"
> Or that I not be in want and steal,
> And profane the name of my God.
> Proverbs 30:8-9

Agur, son of Jakeh wrote this proverb about neither wanting wealth nor poverty. He acknowledges some wealthy people begin trusting their riches but he also recognizes the multitude of challenges among the impoverished. Both financial states have their own trials and temptations, but neither are holier states than the other. This is a balance we need to keep in mind. It is common in our divided nation to pit wealthy against poor. Many will decry the poor as being merely lazy sluggards. Likewise, those poor and lazy sluggards know for a fact they have been oppressed by evil wealthy people. The proverbs are full of people who fell to ruin for spending more than they had by leveraging credit, and other proverbs tell how sluggards will fall to ruin because sleep was more important than the harvest. But the penning of *James 5* gives us examples of ways some wealthy people do indeed oppress the poor.

As we dive into this controversial topic we need to embrace the understanding we cannot determine the state of a person's heart by the presence or absence of material possessions. It is easy to get envious of a person more materially blessed then us, but that does not mean they have accumulated their wealth maliciously. In short, it is our duty to measure our own hearts, not the hearts of others. Reflect on this portion of scripture from the Sermon on the Mount (*Matthew 6:19-21*):

*Do not store up for yourselves treasures on earth, where moth and rust destroy, and where thieves break in and steal. But store up for yourselves treasures in heaven, where neither moth nor rust destroys, and where thieves do not break in or steal; for where your treasure is, there your heart will be also.*

It is our own duty to define our treasure. We all have sentimental belongings and we have material goods that are important to us whether it be time saving devices or just things which bring us joy. That is OK so long as we do not focus on those things to the detriment of Christ in our hearts. Let us examine our own hearts to make sure we are not placing our treasure in material things; rather our focus should be on the Kingdom of Heaven.

The next concept in our balance is one of debt and credit. America has become a debtor's nation not only on the federal level, but also on a personal level. Credit is so aggressively marketed to us that our youth begin receiving credit card advertisements before graduating high school.

In addition, we are trained that we will become homeless bums if we do not attend college, but the costs are so high, we must take out student loans...don't worry! It will be worth it! In fact, I (Tom) remember my college graduation when the university president was talking about the value of our education. He said, "The average person will leave here with a student loan costing $200 per month for the next ten years. That is a good price to pay." I actually thought that very moment, "If this education is so valuable, why will it take so long to pay off?" Of course, we need a car, and a car payment is just a way of life, so let's just buy a car we like and suffer through the payments! As of this writing, the average car payment in America is about $500 per month and the average student loan repayment is way higher than $200 per month! Don't forget your house. And of course, you need to enjoy your life, so sign up for one (or more) streaming services so you can have movies to watch with your expensive, financed television as you relax from the hard day of work while you are trying to pay off everything!

Contrary to the average American life, the scriptures give us a lot of warnings about debt. Some of the more modern translations are comically accurate in saying, It's stupid to guarantee someone else's loan! (*Proverbs 17:18*, CEV). In keeping with our trend of not jumping versions, here are a few warnings from the NASB Bible about credit: *The rich rules over the poor and the borrower becomes the lender's slave (Proverbs 22:7)*. Many verses in Proverbs deal specifically with the concept of co-signing, which is promising to pay a loan for another in the event they cannot pay. If your own debts are a problem to you, certainly never take on a pledge to pay for someone else. You will generally end up paying in the end, but you will only be notified when your credit has already been damaged for non-payment of a loan. Consider these Proverbs:

*My son, if you have become surety for your neighbor,*
*Have given a pledge for a stranger,*
*If you have been snared with the words of your mouth,*

*Have been caught with the words of your mouth,*
*Do this then, my son, and deliver yourself;*
*Since you have come into the hand of your neighbor,*
*Go, humble yourself, and importune your neighbor.*
*Give no sleep to your eyes,*
*Nor slumber to your eyelids;*
*Deliver yourself like a gazelle from the hunter's hand*
*And like a bird from the hand of the fowler.*
*Proverbs 6:1-5*

If you find yourself as a co-signer of a loan, or even in debt of any kind, do not just let it be because you can 'make the payments'. Do what you can to remove the debt from your life. Work extra jobs, go without pleasure spending, cut your life back, become a hermit to things of pleasure until you have paid every cent. Trust us that without debt hanging over our heads we will be a lot happier and even more productive in life. Another proverb reminds us that people who hate borrowing money are more secure (*Proverbs 11:15*). Truly, debt can bind us and it can prevent us from following the path God desires us to walk in.

While debt is a major problem in our world today, it is not the only problem. We have become people who spend without a plan. Often times, spending without a plan is spending on debt, but other times, it is spending money that we do have on things we really do not need or intend to have. This means spending impulsively. *Proverbs 21:5* speaks to this:

*The plans of the diligent lead surely to advantage,*
*But everyone who is hasty comes surely to poverty.*

We should plan our spending and stick to that plan, but of course, that is contrary to what marketers want. They want to get us emotionally stirred up so we spend money we intended to keep. They want us to stop at the upcoming fast food restaurant, or even worse, with tracking included on mobile phones, to give us ads, texts, and notifications when we are in the vicinity of their stores. All this drives us to become more impulsive, and impulsiveness is counter to the balance by which we should live our lives to the glory of God.

While the Israelites settled easily into the worship of false gods like Baal and Moloch, we in the west are equally susceptible to Baal in the form of consumer marketing. We worship iPhones enough to stand in line for days in anticipation only to sign up for a monthly payment plan on a device worth more than our first car. The devices we seek to buy, or sign up for free service, turn us into the product bought and sold. The companies build up psychological profiles on all of us users and use the data to more effectively target their marketing. But the error is not in their court, they are merely providing temptation. We follow through, extend our credit, justify our payments, and sink lower into the stupor of cool consumer entertainment while the still, small voice of God eludes us. It is better to seek Him first and not get involved with the consumer push for the latest thought-children of executives seeking to merely gain profits.

# New Year Revolutions

## TOM'S NEW YEAR

New Year's Eve was one of my favorite holidays. While it meant the Christmas vacation was over, it also meant a night to stay up late (when parents actually enforced bed times on their children). For us it meant late night movies, television, and we always ordered a pizza from John Wildwood's, the best pizza in Erie county. The bonus to New Years included enjoying the evening with friends. Sure, the new year meant we had to be back in school in a day or two, but the relaxing night with pizza, friends, and a late night movie overshadowed our gloom. As for the popular New Year tradition, I was never one to make resolutions and I am not that person today. The only tradition I had in my teen years was to create a mixed tape of my favorite music from the concluding year, so as to lock my memories of the year gone by in song.

## TYLER'S REFLECTION

New years has never held much importance to me. With modern civilization opting for a more monotonous type of living, the 9 to 5, it's hard to differentiate days, weeks, and years. 40 to be exact, — the average person experiences professional work from the ages of 25 to 65. You might switch jobs, upgrade positions, and a variety of adjustments, but anything can feel boring and days can get blurred. My family never had insane celebrations or extravagant events planned either, and that didn't help with my view of the holiday. I don't know much about New Year's and how it should be celebrated. I remember live shows of musicians I like and always look forward to who they're going to bring, but I was (and even now) usually going to bed before the ball drops. As New Years passes, the only thing it signifies for me is the earth getting older.

## A New Beginning

New Year's Eve is often heralded in as an indulgent party in New York City. We grew up on the East Coast and so were brought up with the ball dropping in Time Square; though neither of us have ventured there for the live festivities. New Year's not only marks the beginning of the calendar year, but it is a celebration of the past events, a call to look forward to the future, and the number one time of the year for making resolutions. This chapter discusses the changes to the annual calendar over the years, the beginning of New Year's, and the traditions surrounding this date from antiquity to our modern era.

The new year was not always in the middle of the coldest days of the year, but rather it was usually closer to the spring. Ancient times, particularly of the more 'civilized' agrarian societies, depended on the growing season and a period of rest. The coming of spring, warmer weather, and the approaching growing season usually marked the beginning of the year as it was for the Hebrew nation among others. Of course setting the new year as the start of the growing season was not universal. Some cultures did use the winter solstice a week from our present January 1 as the start of the year since they celebrated the returning of the sun from the lowest point on the horizon. Of course, this was not universal because indigenous peoples were closer to the equator and the sun's position in the sky did not change so noticeably throughout the year.

As we embark on this study of New Years and calendars, we will avoid the complex mathematics often accompanying the creation and evolution of calendars. We will attempt to show the important changes as they relate to how we finally arrived at our modern holiday celebration.

## ANCIENT CALENDARS

Ancient calendars were complicated by shifting patterns of the sun and the moon. The regular, yet different, cyclical patterns of the two celestial bodies lent to some civilizations creating calendars based on the lunar cycles while others focused on solar cycles. Two calendars have been proposed as the oldest. The most agreed upon ancient calendar appears to be a lunar calendar in Scotland. The timepiece is a series of pits in Aberdeenshire which sequentially show the time of the year based on the cycles of the moon. The initial reports of this calendar were made by researchers at the University of Birmingham in 2013[i]. This remarkable calendar is believed to predate the previously known oldest Mesopotamian calendar by 5000 years even more remarkable because the indigenous people who created the calendar were actually hunter gathers rather than agricultural. The pits seemed to function as a device not too dissimilar to a sundial, but they measure moon cycles instead of the shadow of the sun. As could be surmised, each culture had its own calendars making unifying dates difficult, particularly to people who were attempting to engage in business with neighbors.

---

[i]Time and a Place: A luni-solar 'time reckoner' from 8th millennium BC Scotland, *Internet Archaeology*, July 15 2013.

As history progressed, people began developing the calendars we use in our present day: a combination of lunar and solar cycles. The typical antiquities calendars consisted of twelve months because there are twelve lunar cycles for every single solar cycle. This leads to a fascinating question linguists may have about our present naming convention for months because our last four months are named after Seven, Eight, Nine, and Ten!

It turns out the predecessor to our current calendar came from ancient Rome. Romulus who is credited as founding the great city supposedly introduced a calendar consisting of ten months rather than twelve because during those days in Rome, winter months were simply ignored. Of course this approach did not line up with either the solar or the lunar cycles so extra months were added by Numa Pompilius about 40 years later to account for about 60 missing days and to give names to months with the added days. The months were added before the existing ones rather than after for reasons unknown, however, one theory states January was named for the god Janus, which was the ancient god for beginnings and endings. This marks the perfect name for the first month as the beginning is first, but connected to the ending. The second month of February was named for the purification festival, Februa, which was the only significant day in the old monthless second 30 days of winter. Thus, our twelve month calendar with the last months named for seven through ten was born!

During the Classical Greek transitional period, the Roman Empire, the Persians, and the Babylonians rose to power in the old world. They assimilated Greek thought into their cultures. They generally used solar calendars with a great degree of accuracy, but they still only reported 360 day years, so an extra leap month was added every six years to align the solar cycles and the constellations. Though the Babylonians generally used twelve months, their year (along with many other nations) started the year around March at the first new moon after the spring equinox. This was common as an ancient new year because it marked the end of the cold rest and the beginning of the growing season.

As empires united through conquest and Roman peace spread through Asia and Europe, more thought and calculations were made to create a better calendar to unify the expansive Roman empire. In 46 BC, Julius Caesar commissioned what would become the first global calendar, putting his rendition in place January 1, 45BC after adjusting the current year by 60 extra days to adjust for the drifting sun. The day of January 1 was selected in honor of Janus as a means to look back to the old year and forward to the new.

For the technology at the time the calendar was remarkably accurate with each year containing 365.25 days, and a leap year occurred every 4 years adding one more day to the second month. This became known as a Julian Calendar and it was observed by the Roman empire, and eventually through the influence of the Roman Church, it spread throughout the world. The calendar was in regular use from its inception until the medieval church in the 1500s.

## THE CHRISTIAN CONNECTION

As accurate as the Julian calendar kept time from its inception, seasons were still shifting out of sync with the calendar; of particular significance was the calculation of the Easter holiday. It turns out the Julian Calendar was very accurate, but still added an extra day every 128 years requiring further adjustment. By the time of Pope Gregory XIII, the Easter holiday which precisely followed the lunar phases had shifted out of sync with the requirements for the

Easter holiday as laid forth by the Council of Nicaea[i]. Further calculation determined the year was off by ten days.

The Gregorian calendar was created by Luigi Lilio who determined the solar year was closer to 365.242 days rather than the older 365.25 which caused the extra ten days to arrive 1500 years after the creation of the Julian calendar. To account for the days, when the calendar was first introduced, ten days were removed from October. In 1582, October 4th was followed by October 15th to reset the seasons and the equinoxes, but it still was not perfect.

The old Julian calendar included an extra day every 128 years so their leap years corrected some of the shift, but not over a thousand years. The Gregorian calendar by contrast added an extra day every 400 years, so the solution to the drift is eliminating some, but not all of the leap years. This meant the leap year would correct the annual drift if it occurred every fourth year, except the years divisible by 100, except those also divisible by 400. This new calendar with the accompanying leap years will only add an extra day every 3000 or so years, so our modern calendar will be accurate until about 4909 AD.

The Gregorian calendar accomplished one more task: realigning the New Year. While Julius Caesar set January 1st as the date of the new year, this change was not global. Many cultures kept the Winter Solstice or the Spring Equinox as the actual start of the year. The church years generally corresponded to important festivities but it was the decision of the local diocese to determine when the new year would arrive. Pope Gregory XIII officially changed the Roman districts mandating that the new year be reset to January 1st in the whole Roman church. The nations which were under the control of the Roman Church converted instantly, but significant nations including England (and by extension the New World Colonists) did not adopt this date because of

---

[i]While the council did not specify an exact way to calculate Easter, it did officially separate Easter from the Jewish calendar. Easter was thus set on a Sunday following the Equinox that was tied to the new moon.

direct conflict with the Roman Church. They viewed the date change as a conspiracy to stop the protestant church movement. It was not until the mid 1700's the Gregorian calendar was adopted by the British Rule.

Every nation realigning with the Gregorian calendar had to subsequently shift the days to match the new advancing global calendar. In the American Colonies, those days were in September 1752 as Benjamin Franklin was quoted to say:

> And what an indulgence is here, for those who love their pillow to lie down in Peace on the second of this month and not perhaps awake till the morning of the fourteenth[i].

Now, nearly every society has adopted the Gregorian Calendar at least for civil purposes, though some people still accept different new years dates locally (but it does not impact the recorded legal year as it used to).

## CONSUMERISM IN THE NEW YEAR

The modern party started in New York City at the 1907-08 New Year celebration with a 700 pound iron ball that was dropped on a mast in Time Square. The ball drop was not a new idea. Timekeeping was voraciously tracked by mariners by using time balls off the coast of port cities for decades for sailors to use for calibrating their on board chronometers. The port would have a large tower with a ball that would lower every day at a certain time which the lookout on the ship would watch with a spotting scope to calibrate the clocks. One of these time spheres was re-purposed on the reclaimed mast of the USS New Mexico in Time Square.

This display replaced the previous celebrations which included fireworks in the city, but the local law enforcement did not like the idea of flaming ashes pouring over the city so fireworks were banned. Because the previous year

---

[i]Quoted by Cowan, 29; Irwin, 98

celebration was popular in the city, an idea was proposed to combine electricity with the maritime ball drop to celebrate the end of the old year and the beginning of the new. The new tradition began with a 700 pound ball covered in thousands of lights. The popularity of the event drew crowds and increased the budget for the party. The current version of the ball in Time Square is 12,000 pounds and twelve feet in diameter. The celebration draws about a million people annually.

The increased popularity began in 1928 when the festivities were first broadcast on the radio before reaching television in 1956, right after the mainstream adoption of television. This introduced popular arts and culture to New Year's festivities as popular celebrities started making appearances. Once critical mass was realized, marketing and merchandising started to take over and people could buy New Year's glasses, trinkets, hats, banners, and the like to engage in the celebration.

For people who could not attend the party in the Big Apple, other cities and towns created their own traditions. Fireworks are still popular in jurisdictions where they are legal, and most cities including our own State College has an annual party down town which draws a multitude. Arts, shows, bands, and booths arrive in town followed by ice sculptors who carve out of ice statues as marketing tools themselves. Pretzels for the soft pretzel store, a sub for Jersey Mikes, and beer bottles at the local bars. It is a fascinating time of the year, and we as authors do not see any reason to not attend these shows and celebrate the passing of another year.

Towns around America and the world have similar celebrations and traditions. Our real concern is the consumer waste. Neither of us are environmentalists by any stretch, but it is worth discussing that 25% more trash is accumulated over the holiday season. That includes wrapping paper and boxes for those new Christmas gifts, but it also includes the confetti raining down in Time Square during the final decent of the ball. In January 2018, it was reported the confetti officially released was over 3000 pounds in total weight, and the trash crew picked up 50 tons of trash. Obviously, a million people throwing a party in New York City is going to be messy, but our concern is the helliday cropping up around wasteful gadgets used for a single night. In addition to the confetti, this includes the special New Year's party glasses, hats, streamers, light sticks, and the other consumer products purchased that night and discarded before slumber overtakes our eyes.

We will argue in our Christmas chapter that not all spending of money should result in a profitable gain, but we should consider the wastefulness of spending money we rarely have on single use plastic gadgets that will be discarded at the end of the day. We are told by the marketers that we should just 'splurge' because New Year's only comes once a year. This is, of course, their way of getting our money from our wallets and into their coffers while they work on the plan to repeat the process in a few months for the next holiday.

## THE CHURCH'S RESPONSE TO THE HOLIDAY

The New Year is the one holiday the church has widely forgotten, or else they just didn't care to do anything after Christmas week. What started in the Roman days as the celebration of the circumcision right of our Lord (*Leviticus 12:1-8*) has been completely usurped by companies pushing annual parties, favors, and gadgets to ring in the new year. We are left without direction in many churches.

Pastoral direction often remains silent on what to do with New Year's though some call for making resolutions to become better in some way. Usually the only stirring we find is youth group parties, some of which are really good, and others are not so much! The higher quality youth parties should contain some time to think, pray, and reflect over the past year and encourage the kids to develop Godly goals for the year to come.

Godly goals are as simple as reading our Bible and setting goals for prayer; maybe we can include activities such as attending a mission trip, or adding anything to our life to further God's kingdom. This got us thinking: what's the difference between a new year's resolution and goals in the means of grace? Most of the, time new year's resolutions are something to better yourself as a person as though we have just come from a self-help seminar; a nobler motive lies in Godly goals, you're contributing to a bigger picture some believe will come to fruition.

We gathered a few view points and thoughts about how modern pastors are treating this holiday in the church. Billy Graham said this about New Year's:

> Every year, God's people in Old Testament times celebrated the end of the year and the beginning of the new one (just as people of Jewish heritage do today), For most people today, New Year's probably has little religious significance; it only marks the beginning of another year. However, people in Bible times saw the end of the year and the beginning of another very differently[i].

He quotes *Leviticus 23:16* in this speech, which has nothing to do with a new year, but is several months after the Jewish new year, which is fourteen days before the Passover (*Leviticus 23:5*). We appreciate the sentiment he's trying to present, but there is no mention of a New Year's specific holiday the Jewish people celebrated. The better verses for what he was trying to say could be found in *Exodus 12:25-26* which has a hint of reflection in what God commands the adults to tell their children when they ask about the Passover festival; to remember that God brought the Israelites out of Egypt.

---

[i] Billy Graham Applies Faith to New Years' Day; Evangelical Pastor Urges Christians to Give Thanks, *Christian Post*, January 1, 2015

We are not faulting the great ministry or zeal of Billy Graham, but illustrating a bigger error often found in our modern churches: to want to find Bible verse to fit a narrative so bad we cram something in, often out of context or easy to misunderstand. To this end, New Year's is one holiday that really does not even have a glass-darkly of Scriptural basis, though that does not mean it is evil, pagan, and should be ignored by believers. A better illustration would be *Esther 9:27-28* in the midst of the feast of Purim:

> *These days were to be remembered and celebrated throughout every generation, every family, every providence and every city.*

We find a connotation of reflection here. The feast of Purim was celebrated in the Jewish month of Adar, which is equivalent to a February-March time frame. We think it would be good to reflect on New Year's with this type of remembrance undertone rather than trying to fit Scripture into a celebration that did not occur in the Bible.

More concerning to us than self-help messages preached in churches are the teachings among youth during New Year's Eve parties. We found a lesson plan similar to what Tyler had experienced a few times which are popular among youth groups. We will examine such a plan and highlight ways to make it better aligned with Scripture.

This plan comes from a group who creates plans to be used with modern churches, and like most similar plans, they seem to cater to church growth philosophy. The authors suggest everyone is to bring in a favorite Christmas present and discuss what it is, why they like it, and who gave it to them. Of course, this is the 'ice breaker' that is supposed to allow the group to open up to each other. While this isn't inherently wrong, bringing Christmas presents draws attention away from the rest of the lesson. Further, this introduction could alienate some kids who do not have affluent backgrounds and it could lead to some potential covetous behavior.

Second, their program addresses New Year's Resolutions, which is a *commitment* to do something different, but the Bible says this:

> *Nor shall you make an oath by your head, for you cannot make one hair white or black. But let your statement be, 'Yes, yes' or 'No, no'; anything beyond these is of evil (Matthew 5:36-37).*

The whole lesson supports this idea of resolutions, or 'promises', which God rebukes as mentioned in the verse above. New Year's is the time for resolutions according to our world, but God would suggest anytime we mess up we should strive for improvement. Sanctification demands introspection with an emphasis in becoming more like Christ every day, not just when the calendar rolls another year.

We next encounter a disastrous object lesson where a blindfolded person is guided by a voice telling him where a prize is. The blindfolded person is supposed to represent all of us; we cannot see the good things God has for us without listening for the person (God) who can see the prize. The point of the exercise is that God gives us good things eventually in this life, which is not consistent with the Christian faith! Examine what happened to the prophets in *Hebrews 11:35-40* or to Paul as he recounts his journeys in *2 Corinthians 11:22-31*. Consider the general prosecution we shouldn't feel strange facing in *1 Peter 4:12-13*; the only break we are promised is in heaven. When we teach kids God promises good in this life, it sets them up for disappointment and leaves them impatiently waiting for tides to turn. This is one of the main reasons we believe young people are leaving Christianity.

The next section in this study hits the nail right on the head. It addresses Paul, explaining that while he wrote letters in prison even though he knew he might die, he kept his eyes toward God because of the promises kept. This is a great teaching because it focused on always doing the next right things even in the midst of personal trials.

The concluding part of the lesson is commitment cards which we have already addressed above. The cards in this lesson have a covenant prayer inscribed on them. Such cards are common in this type of modern church. They have a Bible verse for in case you are not a Christian and a place to fill in your name to get you to commit to the practices of this plan. While a person could sit into any lesson and become saved, trying to force it does not often lend to sound believers truly devoted to God.

We can fix this lesson in a few ways. First we need to set the stage. Get right into the action of what God says. Kids in youth groups rarely, if ever, need ice breakers, and if they do not know one another, they are better to figure that out on their own. We would probably want to address New Year's resolutions as a cultural thing and lead the kids instead to focus on not needing a new year to change. Use such verses as *Philippians 2:12* to encourage them in their daily walk. We would destroy the idea that God gives us the best earthly life, instead explaining what we could be in for as a Christian. Do not shy away from difficult topics because it is false advertising of Christianity! Finally, leave out commitment cards as they seem to contradict Scripture.

## THE CHRISTIAN'S CALL TO ACTION

The churches responding to the new year often give us little more than sermons on New Year's resolutions, getting fit, improving our lives, and the like. What should be a call to remember the greatness of our God gives way instead to goal settings in our secular life and grabbing more of this world for ourselves. These examples are reminiscent of a church being too close to the culture as a whole, and we believe God would call us to something more.

The call forward requires a look to the past. The Israelite feasts were not the pagan similes contemporary of their day. The pagan call was to please their gods by offering sacrifices, and if the gods were properly pleased, they may be blessed with good crops. To contrast this, the Israelite view meant coming to a holy God with humble knowledge of their sin, and to bring the required sacrifice. When they followed His commandments in obedience, He would bless them with good crops. But the feasts did not have a focus exclusively to the year ahead, they were often a remembrance of the past.

If there were a 'New Year's' celebration in Israel it would be the Passover:

*In the first month, on the fourteenth day of the month at twilight is the LORD'S Passover.*

This was the first feast of the new year, but it was also the most significant Jewish holiday. This was done in the same vein as the New Testament communion: *When you do this, do it in remembrance of Me (Luke 22:19).* The Passover itself began with the Feast of Unleavened Bread and God commanded it as a memorial:

*Now this day will be a memorial to you, and you shall celebrate it as a feast to the LORD; throughout your generations you are to celebrate it as a permanent ordinance (Exodus 12:14).*

The purpose of the memorial is to remember where the Israelites had come from, so they would remember not to go back to foreign gods:

*And when your children say to you, 'What does this rite mean to you?' you shall say, 'It is a Passover sacrifice to the LORD who passed over the houses of the sons of Israel in Egypt when He smote the Egyptians, but spared our homes (Exodus 12:26-27).'*

These feasts, which God commanded the Israelite community to observe, seemed to have the same motivation as Julius Caesar in setting January 1 at the new year: reflection on the past. He looked to the pagan god, Janus, as the god of beginnings and endings; a time to look back to learn from the past, and a time to look forward to have a goal. Of course we should not be worshiping pagan gods, but instead the true God. But God says repeatedly, 'When your children ask why do you do these things...' we must remember the commandments of God. Once we have analyzed the feasts, the commands, the perfect reason for the feast, we are then to look ahead to how to best obey God in our coming year. The Israelites would pray and worship God, obeying Him that blessings would continue (*Deuteronomy 28:1-14*).

As New Testament believers, our New Year should be a time to reflect back on our past year and to think about the year to come. Rather than focusing on the temporal things in our life - our weight or income - the Christian should instead be more focused on improving our overall spiritual well being. The foundation is to remember *2 Peter 1:10*:

*Therefore, brethren, be all the more diligent to make certain about His calling and choosing you; for as long as you practice these things, you will never stumble.*

How does a believer go about diligently making certain about being called by God? It starts with knowing the Bible is our central launching point of instruction:

*All Scripture is inspired by God and profitable for teaching, for reproof, for correction, for training in righteousness; so that the man of God may be adequate, equipped for every good work (2 Timothy 3:16-17).*

Solid Bible study teaches us the mind of God through His revealed Word. Understanding Scripture is a daunting task, but you eat an elephant one bite at a time, and you should never attempt to eat the whole thing at once. Such it is with Bible study. Dedicate a time to study. Some people love the early morning before they start the day, others take time during their lunch break, and some prefer the time right before bed. We do not assume one is any better than the other times, and your preferred study time may certainly change over your life.

Tom, for example, used lunch periods three times per week to get away during graduate school. These periods of time he focused on reading a few chapters and then going through some articles of *Tabletalk Magazine* from Ligonier Ministries. That worked well during graduate school but not as well during the his time as a college professor. During those times, lunches were often times to meet with students for tutoring or grading papers, or building relationships with other faculty. During this period, getting the important Bible study done early in the morning was better. With study out of the way, the rest of the day could be spent in the early stages of building a career. While Tom does not generally do a lot of study during the evening, that is the primary period of study for his mentor who dedicates an hour every night before going to bed. Either method works, as long as it is dedicated time.

Tyler presently finds time before going to bed establishing a micro-habit of reading. He does not do as much focused study time on a personal level because of intense high school studies, but he does find time to study more intensely with a mentor and in Sunday School. Regardless, he tries to complete the Bible cover to cover personally every other year.

As for how we go about studying, we would recommend checking out Tom's book, *Testing and Temptations: A Guide for Sanctification* because it is a guide on how-to methods for studying and growing in the Word.

Second, and equally important area of focus is prayer. This is harder for our personality types because we are more checklist and completion people. For Tom, again, setting aside time attached to study time works best. Another method is to find a special place to pray. It may be a stone or log on a walking trail, a specific place, or even a chair in your house. Dedicate time specifically to pray to God, ask Him to make His Word real to you, pray it back, and seek to align your will to His will. Again, check out *Testing and Temptations* for more specific guidance.

The third area of focus we need to grow as a believer is service. Do not forget we are saved to do good works:

For we are His workmanship, created in Christ Jesus for good works, which God prepared beforehand so that we would walk in them (Ephesians 2:10).

Good service takes on a multitude of forms. Service generally means helping to alleviate the challenges in this world through service rendered to mankind and by sharing the Gospel. Remember the words of Jesus recorded in Matthew 25:34-40:

Then the King will say to those on His right, 'Come, you who are blessed of My Father, inherit the kingdom prepared for you from the foundation of the world. For I was hungry, and you gave Me something to eat; I was thirsty, and you gave Me something to drink; I was a stranger, and you invited Me in; naked, and you clothed Me; I was sick, and you visited Me; I was in prison, and you came to Me.' Then the righteous will answer Him, 'Lord, when did we see You hungry, and feed You, or thirsty, and give You something to drink? And when did we see You a stranger, and invite You in, or naked, and clothe You? When did we see You sick, or in prison, and come to You?' The King will answer and say to them, 'Truly I say to you, to the extent that you did it to one of these brothers of Mine, even the least of them, you did it to Me.'

Service is to serve. That can be in a church function, teaching a Sunday school class, a weekly Bible study, or one of the many programs churches often run. But do not look only to your churches. There are many other places dedicated Christians can, and should, serve. Tom personally spent over 10 years mentoring youth in Big Brother, Big Sisters impacting the lives of dozens of kids who would not otherwise step into a church. Spiritual and secular programs assisting those in need are always looking for volunteers, and we should be ready to step in anywhere God calls us to, whether it be connected to a church organization or not. Just find something you believe would honor God and sign up to do it.

As we start to celebrate the New Year, take some time to reflect on your life in the past and think of how you can improve your walk with God in the year to come. The new year is a time for a new beginning and our beginning should always be to obey God more, follow His commands, and create more fellowship with Him. Augustine also considered the new year and gave his readers this advice[i]:

> Separate yourselves from the heathen, and at the change of the year do the opposite of what they do. They give each other gifts; give ye alms instead. They sing worldly songs; read ye the word of God. They throng the theatre; come ye to the church. They drink themselves drunken; do ye fast.

[i] History of the Christian Church: Nicene and post-Nicene Christianity from Constantine the Great to Gregory the Great, A.D. 311-600, Philip Schaff, Section 77: The Christmas Cycle

# Buy My Valentine

### TOM ON VALENTINES

My earliest memories of Valentine's Day include begrudgingly (think homework) writing down names of everyone in the class on little pink slips of paper purchased from the local K-Mart. I had no clue what the deal was, it was weird to me to even write the boys names on these pink heart-shaped cards, and the feelings were exasperated by the forced jester of kindness towards the kids who spent the whole of nearly every school day teasing me. Don't get me wrong. I enjoyed the mid-class distractions from extra work and the cookies and candies accompanying the day. Thus were my elementary and early middle school Valentine's Days. But as the years progressed, the day morphed into preparation for this holiday in the form of pink grocery aisles that put Barbie to shame. The norms became kissing cams, pink merchandise, and heart-shaped string lights illuminating the porches of overzealous holiday enthusiasts.

## TYLER ON VALENTINES

My view of Valentine's Day has really changed since 6th grade as I grew up and learned more about the natural human inclination to sin, paired with hormonal influences. My Valentine's Day mindset changed drastically, shifting from people showing genuine love to unfettered lust, and I never saw it in the same innocent light again. After I thought about it, I came to a brutal realization as I put the puzzle pieces together: Valentines Day is about two things: selling chocolates and justifying our awful lust for one another. The over-sexualization of women doesn't help my attitude toward this holiday either. Stores are now over advertising chocolates and women are encouraged to be the Valentines gifts to their men on "the day of love".

## THE HEART OF CUPID

Valentine's Day remains shrouded in legend and mystery. Stories of pagan rituals are debated between scholars, believers, and the world at large. February 14th and the surrounding days have history predating Christ, so we start with what we know about the date now rife with roses and candy.

Valentine's Day was a festival dating back to the founding of Rome between 750 and 815 BC by Romulus and Remus. Mythology asserts these brothers were the descendant of either the god Mars or else Hercules. The boys were abandoned as infants but were raised by a she-wolf in a cave called Luprical which became the founding location of their city, Rome.

On this site, the Lupercalia festival was instituted and presided over by the priests bearing the derived name Luperci. In honor of the brothers Romulus and Remus, the festival utilized two noble young men from the aristocratic class every year to partake in sacrificing goats and dogs. The boys were naked except for a loin cloth created from the skins of the sacrificed animals. The attending priest would touch the bloody knife used in the sacrifice to each boy's forehead then wipe off the blood with wool dipped in milk. The remaining animal skins were cut into thongs and the boys would then run through the streets of Rome hitting people with them. The women in particular would line up to be hit because they believed to be touched by the thong would bring fertility in the coming year.

The Lupercalia actually started as a right of purification for the shepherds, of whom Romulus and Remus considered kings. As expected from a sex-centric Roman culture, the festival became a time to honor fertility, and finally it progressed into total sexual gratification. While this time of purification was initially celebrated in Rome during the month of Februarius, it was eventually associated with a Roman god sometimes called 'Februus' in later writings, but no association to such a god is found in the most credible literature. Whatever the intent, the festival spread through much of the empire from the founding of the city of Rome until around 400 AD.

## WHO WAS VALENTINE?

Valentine was a common name during the third century AD, when this holiday was supposedly named. A few priests and teachers were named Valentine, but one was known as a Gnostic teacher and was considered a heretic by the early church fathers. Ironically it is this Valentine whom we know the most about due to the writings of the church fathers whom wrote about his errors. It is likely the histories of the other men whom the holiday seeks to honor have been destroyed. We know there was a Christian named Valentine who was martyred in Africa, but other than those details, we know nothing more. There was also a Valentine who was a bishop of Interamna (Terni) who was martyred and elevated to sainthood after his martyrdom under the Aurelian persecutions, but again, nothing else more is known about this man.

The Valentine usually attributed to this holiday was most likely fictional. He was supposedly a priest in Rome during the reign of Claudius Gothicus (Claudius II). The legend says Claudius banned marriage in the Roman territories to boost the enrollment of the army. He believed people were too focused on their families to be interested in Roman campaigns. Many detractors to the emperor's ban on marriage suggested strong families helped to make warriors motivated to fight in order to stay alive and protect their families. While many priests in Rome during this time obeyed the decree, a priest named Valentine believed God's institute of marriage transcended the law. He believed a strong nation was founded on strong families, and families could only become strong through the God-ordained marriage relationship. As such, Valentine risked the condemnation of the emperor to achieve God's design.

The legend tells that Valentine was eventually imprisoned for continuing to conduct marriage ceremonies. While in prison he befriended the jailer's blind daughter and restored her sight. The legend continues that he wrote her a letter on the eve of his death signing the parchment, 'your Valentine'. The bravery exhibited by Valentine and the validation of the miraculous healing prompted the whole household of the jailer to become Christians.

While this legend is spread far and wide, making resurgences during the second month of every year, we find the silence on this decree from the emperor from the early Christian writings to denounce this as merely a legend. While one source says such a decree to ban marriage was never made by citing letters penned by Claudius to his soldiers instructing them to take a few women each from the females captured during the Gothic conquests, my evidence comes rather from shocking silence. The most notable, accurate, and comprehensive early church historian,

Eusebius, details through ten volumes the early church from the time of Jesus to the conquest of Constantine, his own contemporary. While Eusebius quotes specific names, places, and circumstances for a variety of Christian martyrs particularly in the Roman empire and the happenings of the emperors during this time, no mention of either a decree against marriage or the martyrdom of a priest named Valentine in Rome is ever made in any of his writings. It is also worthy of noting that while Christian persecution was prevalent during this period of the Roman empire, Claudius's reign occurred during a 16 year period of rest from persecution between the time his predecessor declared freedom for Christians and Maxminitus resumed such persecutions 16 years later. Also considering Valentine would have been alive and martyred during the lifetime of Eusebius during the compiling of his text, the absence of this legend from history speaks volumes. We personally denounce this Valentine and his story as pure legend.

## THE VALENTINE CONNECTION

If Valentine was not really a priest as this legend supposes, what really is the history of how Valentine's day became a holiday in the church? The best answer starts with the influence of Christianity in the newly Christianized Roman empire. Constantine did more than merely liberate the Christians; he paved the way for the Roman empire to become a Christian state. Such a change allowed leaders of the church to become officials in positions of power in matters of civil law. As this conversion to Christianity started to inform people, papal powers asserted their own influence.

Several laws banishing pagan worship were passed through the senate inspired by emerging Christian thought. The Lupercalia was one of the last pagan festivals to be removed by decree of law, mostly owing to the fact there was not a well established god presiding over the feast. This leads some historians to assume the Lupercia were probably more of a magical sect than a religious one, but regardless, it was the conduct of the people participating in this festival which finally led to the banishment.

Pope Gelasius I ascended to power in 492, and he quickly began removing the lingering fragments of pagan festivals still celebrated by common people. By this time, the ruling class considered the Lupercalia to be base and primitive, but many of whom were considered the 'rabble' were still celebrating the feast, complete with running naked through the streets. Gelasius penned several letters, one of which is the 100th letter (as numbered by the chronicles) caused final removal of the Lupercalia. Some historians say he replaced it with a celebration of the purification of Mary, which is now celebrated on February 2, 40 days after Christmas to fulfill the time of purification for the birth of a male child (*Leviticus 12:1-4*). The convolution of this matter is the only copy of the 100th letter known is written in Latin and a translation to other languages has not been undertaken. The scholars who have examined the document make no notice of any Valentines connection. The letter to the senate was a mere abolishment of the Lupercalia for religious practices not consistent with Christianity, but makes no mention of a replacement of it with another day of celebration. Furthermore, Gelasius did institute the Feast of the Purification of Mary (Candlemas) but this had no connection with the Lupercalia, rather, the solidification of the churches Christmas celebration during Gelasius's lifetime as December 25th and February 2 is forty days after that date to fulfill the purification of a woman who gives birth to a male child. A celebration of Valentine was never mentioned in his office or writings.

The concepts of both Valentine and Love actually originate in the late 1300's with the famous English poet Geoffrey Chaucer. This influential poet is considered the father of English literature, a primary source of inspiration for Shakespeare, and he is the first poet buried in Poet's

Corner of Westminster Abbey. Chaucer was an emissary of King Richard II, often traveling as his messenger. On his travels to Italy, Chaucer was acquainted with Italian poetry including the stories of the Lupercalia. His famous poem *Parliament of Foules* appears to be the very first historical record of Valentine during this period of time, likely added to create a poetic martyr to an ancient legend of birds finding their mate during the Lupercalia:

> For this was on Seynt Valentynes day,
> Whan every foul cometh ther to chese his make,
> Of every kinde, that men thynke may;
> And that so huge a noyse gan they make,
> That erthe and see, and tree, and every lake
> So ful was, that unnethe was ther space
> For me to stonde, so ful was al the place.
> (309-315)

Other references in the poem include Romulus and the time of purification at the end of winter. These taken together suggest our love connection with modern Valentine's Day seem to start with a poem which influenced many others in England, and it is from English history that we get most of the evidence for our modern Valentine's Day.

Within a century of Chaucer's writings, Charles, Duke of Orleans ascended to power after the assassination of his father. He spent 25 years of his reign imprisoned by the English during the 100 Year's War. From the Tower of London he penned what is considered the oldest existing Valentine:

> *I am already sick of love*
> *My very gentle Valentine...*

His wife died prior to receiving the message, but Charles continued writing. He penned two volumes of work while imprisoned, and his writing tends to lean towards eroticism.

Charles probably set Valentine's Day in stone by writing his *English Book of Love* which begins:

When Nature first created me, says the narrator, she first gave me into the governance of Childhood; later a messenger called Age (in this case something like Growing Up), under orders from Nature, transferred me to the care of Youth. Early on Valentine's Day morning, Youth awakens the narrator and announces that he must go to meet a certain lord. The narrator humbly asks who this may be, but when Youth tells him that it is the God of Love, he declares he is too young and begs to be allowed to put off this service, which he has heard will bring him pain.

This and other excerpts from Charles writings were highly influential in creating the concept of Valentine's Day as we know it today.

Over a century later, Shakespeare used materials from both Chaucer and Charles as inspiration for much of his writing on love. While his plays make several references to love, it is worthy of noting that the Lupercalia also appears in his famous *Julius Caesar*. If Chaucer introduced love sonnets and Charles brought them to the light in both England and France, Shakespeare's work launched love and Valentine into the popular culture making the trend so popular it was finally adopted by the common people.

Another century later and we start to see the consumer impact of Valentine's Day in the *Book of Days*:

Valentine's Day is now almost everywhere a much degenerated festival, the only observance of any note consisting merely of the sending of jocular anonymous letters to parties whom one wishes to quiz, and this confined very much to the humbler classes. The approach of the day is now heralded by the appearance in the printsellers' shop windows of cast numbers of missives calculated for use on this occasion, each generally consisting of a single sheet of paper, on the first page of which is seen some ridiculous coloured caricature of the male or female figure, with a few burlesque verses below. ...the newspapers do not fail to record that the London postmen delivered so many hundred thousand more letters on that day than they do in general. Such is nearly the whole extent of the observances now peculiar to St Valentine's Day.

## BUY MY VALENTINE

In the modern era, store shelves undergo metamorphosis into a heinous pink hue as shopping centers begin priming the pump for Valentine's Day consumption. The helliday is most synonymous with pink candy, heart-shaped boxes, and those pesky little valentines cards which have become all too common in the classroom that to say they are a required text in elementary school is probably not an understatement.

Helliday creep begins with a small shelf dedicated to the earliest of holiday preppers, decorated with the seasonal color, which progressively overtakes other vicinal shelves to dominate a corner of the store. The early products include the cards, candy for the decorative dishes, and random trinkets. By the time the holiday is in full swing we see candies, cards, lights, figurines, and decorated party décor for party sprawl. The stores are ready to sell us, whether by plan or impulse, the things we will need to make it through Valentine's Day without becoming a social outcast.

Our children are not immune from the hustle and bustle of the holiday as the schools will have a time set aside to trade Valentines and consume copious amounts of sugar because the calendar says February 14. Such it is with all of our holidays, though the message remains the same: The point of the holiday is for the store to sell and the customer to buy products wrapped in the spender of the pink helliday hues.

If the grade schools color the holiday bad, the college scene, like usual, is flat out ugly. The hastiness of youth, recently freed from the ruling authority of home rarely marks a difference between love and lust, and the college party scene becomes one of key Valentine's conquests including random kisses and other ungodly passions. Every day can be a day to party, and it is the college groups who often consume more of the party favors than other groups. The pink-themed party dominates the mid-February evenings all in the name of spreading some capital and falling in lust.

Even in the 'real world' as some may call it, the Valentine Creep permeates our minds lending us men to be guilt-ridden should we forget to drop cash on a dozen red roses. Forgetting to take our dates out for a romantic evening is a cardinal sin. We should not expect to survive Valentine's Day without putting out cash for the various trinkets beginning to appear on store shelves immediately following the New Years celebrations.

## ALONE ON VALENTINE'S DAY

Valentine's Day emphasizes couples and the world's different view of love is a little bit too much for me (Tyler). Ever since middle school, moms all over the world keep asking each year "who's your valentine?" or some other variation therein. I don't think it would be far-fetched to say single people are overlooked in this modern landscape, and this feeling only gets amplified around "the season of love" in the days leading up to February 14th.

Me, being a single male in high school feels the full force of this pressure and though I haven't been affected that heavily, a lot of students feel cornered to get a date every February. I've grown defenses and I stick to my pre-decisions. I resolved to never date anyone until I'm ready – mentally, physically and with maturity – and I am the only person who knows when such maturity has occurred. I made this pre-decision when I was in fifth grade and I've kept it up to the day I'm writing this. My mom has insisted I get a girlfriend, I think this is partially due to the cultural mores of today.

The stereotypes associated with being single are partly positive and partly negative: bad at relationships but autonomous, reclusive and antisocial but at least you keep to yourself, these are only some of the adjectives attached to singleness today and some of these were still around in Biblical times. It was quite a different perspective but there's always been a mixed idea of what single people are like. The beginning of *1 Corinthians 7* talks about marital status. While penning the letter, Paul doesn't say one is terrible while elevating the other as holy, but he insists they both have their benefits and drawbacks. Paul describes the married first:

> But because of immoralities, each man is to have his own wife, and each woman is to have her own husband. The husband must fulfill his duty to his wife, and likewise also the wife to her husband. The wife does not have authority over her own body, but the husband does; and likewise also the husband does not have authority over his own body, but the wife does. Stop depriving one another, except by agreement for a time, so that you may devote yourselves to prayer, and come together again so that Satan will not tempt you because of your lack of self-control. But this I say by way of concession, not of command (1 Corinthians 7:2-6).

In Paul's discourse of sex, or more specifically, sexual drive he describes it as a beautiful union displaying holiness when done in the right context, which is marriage. Likewise, Solomon writes prolifically in his Song of Solomon about sex, and the relationship between the newly married young couple. Solomon was not shy of the subject as he encouraged his readers in *Proverbs 5:19* to *enjoy your wife's breasts*. We have discussed the married life, and the Bible isn't opposed. It even promotes sexuality in relationships when in marriage; however, going back to the *1 Corinthians* passage, Paul also addresses singleness:

> *Yet I wish that all men were even as I myself am. However, each man has his own gift from God, one in this manner, and another in that. But I say to the unmarried and to widows that it is good for them if they remain even as I. But if they do not have self-control, let them marry; for it is better to marry than to burn with passion (1 Corinthians 7:7-9).*

His directive is to not be shamed for being single. Paul, being that himself vouches for the like kin by saying that it's been better for him to be without a partner and even wishes that everyone were single.

Paul's exhortation is simple, if we don't have our lust or sexual emotions in check then we should marry because it's worse to be tortured by these desires. There are benefits not mentioned in this section: more time devoted to Christ without a marriage partner and more time to better yourself with the help of God through prayer and personal time. I stay single because I want to focus on God for now. I'm aware of the world I'm growing up in and I want to be prepared for a variety of challenges I know I'll face in the future like saying no to drugs, not to fall when I'm living alone with no filters, how to resist temptations, and just being faithful to Christ. I'm seeing time now as a time to better my future, if God wants to put a girl in my life, then I'll marry, but for now I don't have any desire to date, nor do I have any reason.

## She Has Left Her First Love

Valentine's Day is one of several holidays the modern church has all but forgotten. The only tattered vestiges of this day bearing the name of martyred saints is a dim reflection of the overwhelming commerce in the culture at large. Churches have forgotten the romantic roots of the English writers and either forget this day exists or fully participate as a reflection of the culture. The consumer creep of chocolates, flowers, and hearts have infiltrated the church as she bows down to the Baals of Western consumerism.

While ignoring the history of a holiday named for a martyred Christian saint, some churches use the cultural buzz as Valentine's dinner fund raisers pitched as a date night between couples as a means to hopefully re-spark the courtship felt early in the marriage. This is not inherently problematic, but we argue should be tempered with a better understanding of what love really is. Truly strong families are the backbone of strong churches, and those who can strengthen the families year-round without the help of the local super-mart will have a better handle on the true meaning of the holidays. Regardless, the fact so many churches participate in the sanitized Christian versions of the cultural parties while forgetting the holiday's roots is akin to the frightening message to the church in Ephesus:

> *But I have this against you, that you have left your first love (Revelation 2:4).*

Nevertheless, we can get behind a message calling us to love one another as Christ loves the church and a date night once a year is better than none at all. It does not do any good for our congregations to see the cultural expression of Valentine's Day while the church remains silent. But it is equally appalling for the church to just become the culture by producing sanitized versions of the festivities the world celebrates. So what is the answer?

To address that, we need to know what love really is. Is Love to give roses and a box of chocolates? I know the vendors on Valentines Day love that! But, seriously, love is complicated in the English language because we have one word where the original Greek use four words to describe the various feelings. We use the word translated from *phileo* most of all. This means the affection of friends, and is the word we often use when speaking of foods, entertainment, or other pleasurable things to us. We do not love our ice cream in the same manner we love our families. Speaking of family, there is a Greek word, s*torge*, which is the type of love for family members. Good marriages have *storge* love, a type of deeper friendship than the former, but this is also the type of dedicated love reserved for brothers and sisters, parents and children, and other really close, but not close with sexual intimacy. *Eros*, however, is the love of sexual intimacy. It has no other context in the Greek language than a sexual encounter which expresses love. The final love, that which Christians are called to have, which God has for us is *agape*. This is self-sacrificing love that values other people above ourselves. We are called ultimately to *agape* love with our Christian brothers and sisters, our family, and the world at large.

## Finding the Heart of Valentine

The best thing the church can do is respond to the culture. We need to take an approach beginning with correct understanding of the holiday. For the days bearing a saints name we should start by asking who that person was and what was the cause for their honor. Even in the case of Saint Valentine it is worth knowing there were martyrs bearing his name, but we also need to understand the legend and lore. While I am not one inclined on repeating legends as truth, the reality is a love connection has been made with February 14th every year and so the church needs to take the time to reflect on how to express love.

We need to start by understanding the difference between love and lust and teaching the culture to know the difference. As the culture has so decidedly given us candy and flowers, we as the church need to stand up to suggest love is more than gifts, but rather a reflection of our commitment to one another. While the culture is busy convincing us we need to love, the church should stand up to proclaim real love and describe how it differs from the world's corrupting definition. We do not start with self-love as Robert Schuller and other psychology-based tele-vangelists suggest we should, nor do we focus first on our spouse as does *The Five Love Languages*. Our focus should be fixed on Christ alone as the beginning of love:

> *Therefore, since we have so great a cloud of witnesses surrounding us, let us also lay aside every encumbrance and the sin which so easily entangles us, and let us run with endurance the race that is set before us, fixing our eyes on Jesus, the author and perfecter of faith, who for the joy set before Him endured the cross, despising the shame, and has sat down at the right hand of the throne of God. For consider Him who has endured such hostility by sinners against Himself, so that you will not grow weary and lose heart (Hebrews 12:1-3).*

Jesus came for the sole purpose to die on the cross for us. While our society crumbles into lust-driven, excessively pink Valentine's parties, remember the words of Jesus about how we should relate to one another:

> *This is My commandment, that you love one another, just as I have loved you. Greater love has no one than this, that one lay down his life for his friends (John 15:12-13).*

Jesus did lay down His life for us. He died that we may live. He called us to love each other whether we are saved or not. He called us to a higher calling and enabled us to love without receiving anything in return. In Christ we find freedom.

Regarding marriage relationships, Jesus correlates His relationship with the church with the manner a man should love his wife:

> *Husbands, love your wives, just as Christ also loved the church and gave Himself up for her, so that He might sanctify her, having cleansed her by the washing of water with the word, that He might present to Himself the church in all her glory, having no spot or wrinkle or any such thing; but that she would be holy and blameless. So husbands*

*ought also to love their own wives as their own bodies. He who loves his own wife loves himself; for no one ever hated his own flesh, but nourishes and cherishes it, just as Christ also does the church, because we are members of His body (Ephesians 5:25-30).*

The words of Jesus are not focused on lust or sex. They are not callous, but poignant. As we treat our bodies, keeping ourselves out of harm's way and nourishing ourselves, so we should treat our spouses. This means we self-sacrifice to not endanger ourselves with gluttonous pleasures. We put off Godless pleasure and exchange it for righteousness, and we seek to encourage others in their own righteousness. Yes, love is more than lust. It is more than pleasure; it is to direct a person in the direction of holiness and sanctification that they may honor God with their bodies.

As our love begins to fade from *eros*, or sexual love to *agape*, or devoted love, we see in our life a calming reflection of Christ. This is sanctification. We begin seeing the greater good in mankind as presented to us in Christ. While He did not come to make bad people good, the man or woman who rises from their reprobate grave begins to see the world in a new light. Grace begins to take hold in their life and people take a greater priority than pleasure. This is what love is, and this is the love which caused martyrs to march on to their death for the cause of Christ.

## TAKING IT TO HEART

The Christian's focus on Valentine's Day should be one of denying the consumer creep in this Helliday. As believers we need to be the salt and the light to our fallen world:

*You are the salt of the earth; but if the salt has become tasteless, how can it be made salty again? It is no longer good for anything, except to be thrown out and trampled under foot by men (Matthew 5:13).*

*You are the light of the world. A city set on a hill cannot be hidden; nor does anyone light a lamp and put it under a basket, but on the lampstand, and it gives light to all who are in the house. Let your light shine before men in such a way that they may see your good works, and glorify your Father who is in heaven (Matthew 5:14-16).*

In the context of Valentine's day this means we act in ways honoring Christ in what we do. We choose to accept invitations to parties and gatherings bringing honor to Christ and the family. We need not separate ourselves from festivities of the day, but we are probably best to avoid rampant consumerism. It is also wise to take time during the holiday to focus on how we can better honor our God and our family every day.

The day could also be a cause to engage in conversations about the Saint of its namesake. While I believe the historical evidence is lacking for the traditional Valentine's martyrdom it is not a cause to be throwing out the day all together. Anything can be used as a conversation starter to bring someone into a conversation about why we do all this. Taken together, to convert this helliday to a holiday in our life, we should focus on differentiating the various types of love and reflecting first on the love Christ has for us, then on how we can love our families and neighbors. Rather than becoming a slave to the consumer mindset we should instead focus on what is important.

# A Pinch for Not Drinking Green

### TOM'S THOUGHTS ON SAINT PATRICK'S DAY

"Why aren't you wearing green?" my mother asked as I was getting ready to leave for school in 3rd grade. I was baffled, "why should I wear green" I thought. "It's St. Patrick's Day!" This was technically a reason, but not one I understood. Such was my first memory of St. Patrick's Day, all from the house of a total atheist. Why did our house care about some saint? At school it was not much better. Green cupcakes, green koolaid...green...green...green...why? No one ever talked about a great saint, no one seemed to care; it was merely a day dedicated to the god of green. Of course as time went on, consumer creep bled into green displays across stores, and the college town where I presently reside celebrates Saint Patrick with drunken debauchery induced by green beer...and no one in this present age knows why.

### TYLER'S THOUGHTS ON SAINT PATRICK'S DAY

Saint Patrick's Day, in my opinion, is one of the most useless holidays. When you think about it, this "helliday" presently involves selling crappy green beer and getting drunk. Saint Patrick's Day is a perfect example of what happens when the culture inserts their own new age worldview into a cultural tradition. The holiday is progressively losing its meaning with each passing year. Living in a college town, I see each weekend is now always Saint Patrick's Day, another excuse to engage in excessive drinking. The college students, to some extent, live their lives in drunken monotony. Ever since I was born, this is all I've known it to be, and it's sad because there's nothing "Saintly" about drinking away your pain or trying to fit in with the popular crowd with alcohol.

## THE FORGOTTEN SAINT

Among the various curious holidays in our culture we find Saint Patrick's Day shrouded in mystery. This holiday fascinates me because the Patrick of its namesake is one of the only ancient saints of whom we actually have written historical records about his accomplishments, though parts of his life remain a mystery. Even what we know is rarely discussed in church, but kids are told to wear green or they may be pinched. Outside of the excuse, "It's Saint Patrick's Day" no one seems to know what the day means, and if you ask the college students and fast-food enthusiasts, it means green versions of their favorite beverages are available. Truly this is the most dysfunctional holiday of all because it is named for a great saint who is totally forgotten by the church. It is remembered by schools who talk about wearing green, but these institutions are not legally allowed to discuss the origins of this brief holiday. It is talked of by McDonald's because it gives them an excuse to sell the infamous Shamrock Shake®[i] and colleges around America become stained green by all the food coloring tainting the beer served near campus. The stores remember this day because they boost sales with shamrock paraphernalia, but the church remains silent.

---

[i]Shamrock Shake is a trademark of the McDonald's Corporation

Sadly, and like most holidays, Saint Patrick's Day has been turned into a Helliday; an occasion to gorge ourselves in sin, and in my town alcoholism runs rampant on Saint Patrick's Day, after all, the Irish drink as we are told. Any occasion now found to commercialize any day is rapidly exploited in our age, and March 17<sup>th</sup> is no exception.

## WHO WAS SAINT PATRICK?

While Patrick is associated with Ireland, he was actually from the British Isles, possibly the northern territories close to Scotland. The Isles were under Roman authority during his lifetime and taken together with Patrick's writings, he was a proud Roman citizen, though it is not likely he had any direct experience with Rome. The British Isles were on the fringes of the empire leaving very few Roman soldiers stationed on the island making the area rife with raids from the surrounding countries.

As for exact dates, there is confusion owing to the lack of written history during the Dark Ages, but it is further convoluted by Roman hagiographers who set forth to create a life history of a man without much written history. From his writings we guess he was born around 385 based on his escape from captivity at age 22 around the year 407. It is believed he entered his missionary work in Ireland around 432, but again, it is mostly guesswork. His death is accepted as either 461 or 493, but the day of March 17<sup>th</sup> is generally undisputed.

We know Patrick was a 5<sup>th</sup> century British Christian at least the third Christian in his family line and was likely heavily influenced by the burgeoning Roman Catholic church. In his writings he describes his grandfather as a priest and his father a deacon of the local church. The title of priest was appointed from the bishops of the area under the authority of Rome. He was a member of the clergy class of citizens and as such Patrick was likely educated in his youth more so than many of his peers, but he lost later formal education because of his captivity. His writings demonstrate a man who can reason and write well, but without the formal education of a Roman-sanctioned priest. Despite Patrick's Christian lessons and upbringing at home, he was a very disobedient young man and he believed his early life tragedies were decreed by God to convert him to Christianity.

Patrick became intimately acquainted with Ireland when he was taken captive. The Irish would often raid the British Islands taking prisoners as slaves and Patrick found himself at one such slave auction being sold as a shepherd in his mid teenage years. This was a blessing for Patrick because lonely times on the hills shepherding his master's flock gave him time to reminisce on the teachings about Christ he learned from his family who were dedicated to Christ. He rededicated his life to Christ on those lonely hills and awaited his mission from God while intensely praying. Eventually he received a vision from God showing the image of a ship awaiting his arrival. Patrick left his master's house to follow his vision and boarded the very ship in his visions leaving Ireland around the age of 22. He returned to his village and was reunited with his family.

Patrick became a stranger to both is old life in England but also to his new life in Ireland. He learned of the Irish culture, which was neither written nor savage. They had Roman trading ports and even some population of Christians, though it is unclear to what extent believers were on the island. The work in Ireland included farming of which Patrick was sold into as a slave. Local trading included metal-work and other ancient occupations. The island boasted trade economies and social classes, but many people were simple farmers though archaeology suggests a wealthy class was also present on the island.

We know from Patrick's writings that Ireland was a majority pagan territory. He was called by God to reach the island for Christ as was reported in his writings. Despite being mostly pagan, the island did have a small pocket of Christians. The island had trade routes with Rome, and we have written record that Pope Celestine sent a priest or bishop by the name of Palladius to Ireland, but history suggests he never arrived. God determined Patrick, not Palladius, to be His missionary to the island.

## THE GREAT ESCAPE

During his years of captivity, Patrick grew closer to God. He prayed several times throughout the day and into the night about what he might do for the almighty. One day he received a heavenly vision of a ship and set out from his master's house, walking several hundred miles to find the ship in his vision. He spent three days at sea before setting foot on British land once again. He described his homeland as a desert, though we are unsure if this was ruins of the land from the raids or if this was more of a spiritual description. After about a month of wandering Britain he returned home to find his family alive.

After returning to his home country, Patrick, received three more visions: one of a messenger carrying many letters with the same inscription "*O holy boy, we beg you to come again and walk among us.*" He then received another call, "*He who gave His life for you, He who it is that speaks to you.*" And the rest of that message was not clear. He then received another internal call including a vision of God the Spirit praying for him, which finally compelled him to return to Ireland to be once again a stranger in a strange land.

Patrick returned to Ireland between 432 and 435, presumably after receiving some kind of learning, though it is uncertain if or where he was educated. Patrick was a knowledgeable and persuasive Christian to both the common people and the wealthy class.

During the short period of time he administered the Gospel in Ireland, the religious shift in the island was dramatic. He is known as "The Apostle to Ireland" because he baptized thousands of men, was described as the most zealous and efficient evangelist, and performed many miracles across the countryside. He conquered the Druids of the island, and even battled the slave trade as described in one of his two surviving documents. Patrick became the human instrument by which God converted the entire island of Ireland from Celtic druidism, barbarism, and idol worship to Christianity. Patrick is credited with the foundation of 365-700 churches and he consecrated around 3000 Irish priests in addition to the unnumbered thousands of people that were baptized. He changed the laws of the kingdom, healed the blind, and he raised nine people from the dead. That is what we call an effective Christian!

## PATRICK THROUGH TIME

Despite Patrick having one of the most fruitful ministries of early western Christianity, he was mostly unknown because he lived on the fringes of the Roman empire and served in a non-empire state. It is also significant his lifetime was the start of the collapse of the Roman Empire. He was, however, known among the Irish Christians, but his story does not unfold until about the eighth to twelfth centuries when the Roman Catholic church was creating a man to celebrate as the saint of Ireland.

During this period of time, a lot of the legend surrounding Patrick arose. The Roman biographers would often create more fanciful Christians as heroes for the common people to look up to, not unlike famous movie stars today. Regardless, most of the truthful history comes from Patrick's own writings, which appears to have been unknown to the hagiographers. Regardless, Patrick became known to the world again through the Catholic tradition and March 17th became a day to celebrate, mostly by parading in the streets.

With the inclusion in Roman history, Patrick would not be forgotten from the church, but matters of general society were another order. The observation of Saint Patrick gained notoriety in politics when Irish influence began to spread in Britain. Wanting to appease some of the Irish sojourning in the Islands, George III signed the statutes instituting the Order of Saint Patrick, a knighthood, in 1783 which was to help garner political support among the Irish citizens. The symbols of this knighthood became the red cross of Saint Patrick, a gold harp, and most importantly, the shamrock (which of note is three leaflets, not four – Patrick used the symbol to teach the trinity). This knighthood does not specifically celebrate Saint Patrick's Day, but it's creation brought awareness to the pre-existing celebrations

Patrick was claimed, at least in name, by the Roman church and the British government, both of which added his name into celebrations containing very little history outside of a parade in the streets. Being a prominent day in Ireland by default and Britain by inference, it is no wonder this day of short celebration is included on our modern calendars, it is probably the poitín that put it there.

Poitín is an Irish whiskey that became common sometime during the dark ages. Some have said Patrick taught the people how to create the distilleries, but that seems more legendarily trying to validate alcohol consumption. It is further discredited by the fact Patrick taught temperance including to abstain from drinking most of the time (though in the evening it was permitted). Regardless of the origin, alcohol distillation became so widespread and problematic that it became regulated as early as 1556 which first introduced the requirement of a license to distill alcohol. It is not such a surprise alcohol became synonymous with Irish spirit and Saint Patrick's Day.

## THE DEVOLUTION OF A DAY

Patrick was truly an amazing saint. He was not sent by a counsel, yet he listened to a calling from God Himself. Any of us would not think a man less for hating people who violently captured us nor would we find compassion for those people who enslaved us, but Patrick set aside any malice of his past and preached, out of love, to the very people who had done him so much harm. This is truly a man worthy of celebration, but how does a holiday devolve from a celebration of a Christian saint to merely wearing – and drinking – green products. What happened to cause such a proliferation of green beer, milkshakes, and other cultural paraphernalia while the true story of saving grace is long forgotten? We hope to address these things in the rest of our time in this chapter.

In American culture, Saint Patrick's Day was celebrated since the late 1700's, but from protestants wishing to honor their homeland rather than as a religious festival. This was different from the Catholic celebration which would have been blasphemous to the puritans in Boston where the first records of the celebration occurred.

Saint Patrick's Day was not recognized as a national holiday, so it was routinely held on the nearest weekend to March 17th, but that changed in Savannah, Georgia when that date was set as the official day for the parade regardless of the day of the week. While even still today it is not a national holiday, Saint Patrick's Day is recognized as a time to honor Irish pride even among non-Irish people, but more often than not it is a day set aside to worship the color green in the form of clothing, Shamrock Shakes, and green beer. Several cities dye fountains, rivers, and even buildings green in honor of Saint Patrick's Day.

The association with alcohol may relate to the poitín we described above, but that intensified when the Catholic church declared a person may have an exclusion for not drinking alcohol on Lent. Thus when church started embracing alcohol consumption on Saint Patrick's Day it cemented the commercialization of booze forever.

## STATE PATRICK'S DAY

Debuting in 2007, State Patty's Day was started by a Facebook group who noticed Saint Patrick's Day usually occurs over spring break on the Penn State University academic calendar. Due to our narcissistic nature as humans and the popularity of partying on college campuses, this group made State Patrick's Day a disgrace of all previous Christian values. To digest why this is such a big problem and how it came about, we need to look at the root: a shift in college focus around the country from academics to being "all about the experience", which for some includes copious amounts of beer and sexual conquests. Thus, the new "State Patrick's Day" was created to totally usurp a classic holiday.

As drinking and Saint Patrick's Day were cemented by the Catholic church as described above, it is no surprise college groups would latch onto that. People used to drink to celebrate all of the accomplishments of Saint Patrick, but as with most things that pass with time, our corrupt nature, and our very selective memory caused us to forgot the good tradition and latch onto the sinful one. Not only are we disrespecting Saint Patrick in this scenario, but we are also disgracing God, reducing His magnificent works and faithful servant to a drinking holiday. This isn't bad just from a Christian standpoint, this is also from a secular view. Consider the effects on future generations, what this teaches them about both how to act in college and how to act when they're just grown up in general, not only that, but what effect could this have on other holidays?

Nothing good can come of this, whether we are observing or participating, so we choose to not be a part in it at all. In the fallout of this helliday, more problems have been occurring downtown State College, PA causing Tom

Fontaine and Damon Sims, the borough manager and Student Affairs vice president respectively, to issue a 2011 letter to all restaurants, pubs and places of the like to "avoid drinking specials" because the arrests that year were "climbing over 400[i]". Looking at the statistics, his letter did have a positive ripple effect. According to the State College Local News, arrests went down 177 reported from the prior year and calls decreased by 185 reported incidents[ii].

The original celebration made a big deal about praising God and remembering Saint Patrick for his wonderful works, converting Ireland from druidism into a Christian nation. There was a feast and a large scale public festival or parade as well, and Christians were able to drink to the celebration of Saint Patrick's achievements. Lent was a Christian preparation that took place 40 days before the Easter celebration in which the church restricted pleasurable expression. Saint Patrick's Day fell right in the middle of Lent and because the church could not contain the celebrations, they acquiesced, lifting the ban on this day leading it to be a party day. The festivities would end and they would drink a 3 leaf clover with alcohol for good luck and a toast for Saint Patrick.

North America only adapted certain parts of the holiday, and though it did start as a more traditional holiday, ultimately, it devolved into a drinking helliday devoid of roots we know today. The way stores market "wear green or get pinched" and the way bars market the "green beer only available for a limited time" is both clever and trickery to bring in more customers. It raised a lot of hell and made a lot of bars happy. The predicted amount of money that will be spent on this day (in 2018) will be $5.92 billion up from the previous $5.27 billion in 2017, In 2016, $4.4 billion[iii] was spent, even by numbers, this is getting

---

[i] 'None of us want those outcomes.' How Penn State and State College prepare for State Patty's Day, *Centre Daily Times*, February 22, 2018
[ii] State Patty's Day Sees Increase in Arrest Numbers, Decrease in Total Reported Crime, *StateCollege.com*, March 2, 2018

worse. We think the best way to avoid any complications this year during State Patrick's Day is to not go into town at all.

## CONSPIRACY TO SELL GREEN

As a young man I (Tom) do not recall anything more to Saint Patrick's Day than a commandment to wear green. Somewhere around college I started seeing the proliferation of green paraphernalia in various stores. The corner of local big box stores began shifting from pink to green in the effort to tempt the passers-by with spending 99 cents more to make their dwelling more festive. And let us not forget the shame of those people who neglect their green hats, shirts, and beverages. Green dye and food coloring spike the economy and now every store starts selling cheap green junk in the name of holiday consumerism. Whether it is the sugar cookies with shamrock shaped green colors or McDonald's famous Shamrock shake®. Grocery store shelves are filled to the brim with green cookies, candies, and small trinkets.

Like Valentine's Day, Saint Patrick's Day was not initially one of the commonly celebrated holidays, probably owning to the initial limited celebrations in the Irish communities, but once the Irish in Boston and Savannah mainstreamed their parades, the wheels of consumerism started spinning. Eventually the American way of celebrating the holiday was back-ported to Ireland so they now celebrate with parades like Americans instead of attending the church services of the past.

In the wake of these parades, green hats, necklaces, and other benign trinkets began to be marketed to the younger crowds while college towns across the country started to celebrate with green colored beer. What started as a few cards and general policies about wearing green turned once again into full-blown decorations, strings of lights, cards,

---

[iii]St. Patrick's Day, Holiday and Seasonal Trends, *National Retail Federation*, Accessed May 2019

candies, stickers, all with shamrocks and other green threads. The National Retail Federation has tracked holiday spending since 2007, and Saint Patrick's Day has grown in spending every year with an estimated $5.9 Billion in American spending on this day alone, with nearly a quarter of the adults heading to a restaurant or bar for a Saint Patrick's Day party. It is true we overspend on a day the average American knows nothing about the foundation thereof.

## THE CHURCH'S RESPONSE

Patrick was truly a powerful saint but while our secular calendars announce the March 17th holiday, our local stores celebrate the accumulation of our green money for their green widgets. The protestant church is utterly silent in all this while the Catholic tradition still venerates this amazing man, but the rest of Christendom has let the pagan world pollute the helliday without a mere mention. How can we recapture this day to bring honor and glory to God? We think the best approach is one of remembrance.

Two sections of Scripture give us a call for remembrance:

*For the LORD will pass through to smite the Egyptians; and when He sees the blood on the lintel and on the two doorposts, the LORD will pass over the door and will not allow the destroyer to come in to your houses to smite you. And you shall observe this event as an ordinance for you and your children forever. When you enter the land which the LORD will give you, as He has promised, you shall observe this rite. And when your children say to you, 'What does this rite mean to you?' you shall say, 'It is a Passover sacrifice to the LORD who passed over the houses of the sons of Israel in Egypt when He smote the Egyptians, but spared our homes.'" – Exodus 12:23-27*

*So Joshua called the twelve men whom he had appointed from the sons of Israel, one man from each tribe; and Joshua said to them, "Cross again to the ark of the LORD your God into the middle of the Jordan, and each of you take up a stone on his shoulder, according to the number of the tribes of the sons of Israel. Let this be a sign among you, so that when your children ask later, saying, 'What do these stones mean to you?' then you shall say to them, 'Because the waters of the Jordan were cut off before the ark of the covenant of the LORD; when it crossed the Jordan, the waters of the Jordan were cut off.' So these stones shall become a memorial to the sons of Israel forever." – Joshua 4:4-7*

In these two scriptures, God commanded the Israelites to establish a memorial. This is a lesson to the Israelites to remember where they came from to gain a better focus on where they are going. As Christians in our modern age, we need to remember our past as well. Patrick's own life echoed that sentiment as he was a man called to a land that enslaved him, his past life as a memory for where he would go. He remembered his old life in England and his enslaved life in Ireland. Ultimately he learned to hear God during his earthly slavery and then subjected himself to the slave labor of God.

Like Patrick, we need to start with remembering what he and other great saints have done. Then we need to remember Patrick believed he was in the end times, and he lived like it. He preached the Gospel, brought people back to Christ and the cross, and taught the Irish how to live by the Scriptures. For this reason, I (Tom) generally do not wear green on Saint Patrick's Day because someone will invariably inquire as to my lack of a green wardrobe, giving me a conversation starter to ask why they are celebrating this great saint.

Taking this approach, the church might be best to remember the fallen saints and talk about who they are and what they did for God's Kingdom. Saint Patrick can be used as a springboard to point back to what this and other saints have done over the days to remember the result of bold people standing for God. We are thus commanded not to have a spirit of timidity but to boldly proclaim the life and purpose of Christ, following the examples of the great saints.

Paul gives this instruction to his disciple, Timothy:

*For God has not given us a spirit of timidity, but of power and love and discipline (2 Timothy 1:7).*

We see we do not have fear, so us Christians need not recoil from the drunken consumerism of the culture surrounding us, but rather, like Patrick, we should confront it. When we confront the world, we take our cue from Paul's instruction. First, we confront the culture with power. We talk about the power of God, which is a humble meekness placing our faith in Him rather than our ability. Second, we confront the culture with love. This is difficult in our time when many dissenters will declare mere disagreement actually implies we hate people holding opposing views to our own. That is not truth, and truth means we love the world, saved or not, regardless of their sin. We do not need to celebrate their sin, but give love and dignity to all. Finally we confront the culture with discipline (*2 Peter 1:5-7*). We know our own limits and seek to live a disciplined life to show the world we are able to hold fast to the commands Christ gives His people. We are to abstain where we ought to abstain, consume where we ought to consume, and live our life in moderate discipline.

These three key points were the core of Patrick's life as he confronted pagan Ireland as a foreigner and conquered the old way of worship while preaching temperance, love, and the supreme power of God. Let us live that same way, looking to the past for the example of how to live in the future.

We conclude with a portion of a prayer that is allegedly written by Patrick before he confronted the chief ruler of Ireland which is now known as the Breastplate of Saint Patrick:

I bind myself today, –
To the power of God to guide me,
The might of God to uphold me,
The wisdom of God to teach me,
The eye of God to watch over me,
The ear of God to bear me,
The Word of God to speak for me,
The hand of God to protect me,
The way of God to lie before me,
The shield of God to shelter me,
The host of God to defend me

Christ with me, Christ before me,
Christ behind me, Christ within me,
Christ beneath me, Christ above me,
Christ at my right, Christ at my left,
Christ in breadth, Christ in length, Christ in height
Christ in the heart of every man who thinks of me,
Christ in the mouth of every man who speaks to me,
Christ in the eye of every man that sees me,
Christ in the ear of every man who hears me –
Salvation is the Lord's,
Salvation is the Lord's,
Salvation is Christ's,
Let thy salvation, O Lord, be ever with us.

# The Bunny and the Tomb

## TOM'S EASTER MEMORIES

Late February 1985 we packed up one small bag each of clothes and toys and ran away from our home in Nevada. My mother had met a guy who drove us across the United States back to her home state of Pennsylvania where we lived at a cousin's house in a small town more populated by cows than people. Only one month later in early April we walked to a church for the first Easter service I ever attended. Like many secular Americans at that time, my Aunt and Uncle went to church on Easter and Christmas, but they were not otherwise Christian, so we still had no instruction in Christianity. As we sung the songs so common on Easter I asked my mother who God is, but she said she didn't know and not to ask again, and such was my upbringing in faith until my twenties when Jesus came and found me. Like all Easter Sundays of my childhood, it was not a day to worship a risen Savior, but rather a day to find a basket full of candy and small toys. This first Easter I received a Lego set and new camouflage Pajamas. Future Easter Sundays would be days of looking for a basket, getting gifts, and not knowing or hearing anything about Jesus. It would be several more years before I even heard what Easter was actually about.

## TYLER'S EASTER MEMORIES

When I was young, all I remember was receiving gifts on Easter; mainly candy. We also had a good Easter-centric church service, but to me and my young peers, that was always the third wheel when it came to the Easter celebration. Now in my late teens I don't value Easter Baskets as much as I used to. I'm obviously more observative than I was as a child and when I think about consumerism, I remember a lot of marketing, but the amount of adverts and decorations in stores has been exponentially increasing. In my opinion, Easter is yet another holiday that lost all value because of over-commercialization. It's an excuse to get all of the left over candy into our hands because consumerism implanted this fairly new tradition of candy baskets into all future generations.

## THE ONE TRUE CHRISTIAN HOLIDAY

Of all the holidays celebrated in our modern culture among Christians, Easter is the only one with an absolute connection back to New Testament believers. Not that it has remained pure from the pagan influences throughout the ages, but if there is one holiday no Christian should take up their cross against, it is Easter. The question becomes one of purpose and practice. Is it Biblical? Should we hide Easter eggs or mention an Easter Bunny? These are the questions we seek to explore in this chapter.

Before we talk about how Peter Cottontail hopped out of an empty tomb, we also need to make a solid connection between Easter and the Old Testament. We have detailed in our Appendix all the holidays required of the Jewish nation. Easter is specifically about the resurrection of our Lord, which was the culmination of events surrounding the

Jewish Passover. The message from the Bible is very clear: Jesus is the new covering for the sin of the nations, and being covered in the New Passover Blood in Christ we have covering and propitiation for our sins.

It was Easter itself that managed to change the day of worship from Saturday, the day of the Sabbath, to Sunday, the day our Lord rose from the dead. Christians through the ages have set aside Sunday for the weekly remembrance of the day Jesus rose from the grave. Easter, however, is the specific day Jesus rose, and that makes it of more importance than any typical weekly Sunday.

There is not a specific Biblical command in the New Testament to celebrate Easter but the tradition of the holiday predates the councils, was already moving in the second century church, and therefore was likely established in the apostolic age. Some Scriptures even reference possible connections to Easter festivities including *1 Corinthians 5:7-8*:

> *Clean out the old leaven so that you may be a new lump, just as you are in fact unleavened. For Christ our Passover also has been sacrificed. Therefore let us celebrate the feast, not with old leaven, nor with the leaven of malice and wickedness, but with the unleavened bread of sincerity and truth.*

This verse indicates the importance of Christ as the Passover lamb, and connects a celebration in the newly established Christian church with the events of the Jewish Passover.

Other scriptural indications include a few passages in Acts where Paul is possibly traveling around the festivals generally connected with Easter:

> *Acts 20:6 – We sailed from Philippi after the days of Unleavened Bread, and came to them at Troas within five days; and there we stayed seven days.*

*Acts 20:16 – For Paul had decided to sail past Ephesus so that he would not have to spend time in Asia; for he was hurrying to be in Jerusalem, if possible, on the day of Pentecost.*

These verses together with historical records of Easter combined with the fact Easter is a holiday based on the lunar calendar and not the solar calendar, all taken together to indicate the Easter tradition is truly the only holiday we celebrate that is directly connected to the Scriptures[i]. Of course, the celebration of Easter was not without the interference of the church. Our modern celebration corresponds to the Roman church setting of Easter on a Sunday, but the church fathers may have disagreed with a Sunday placement. In a great debate between Polycarp (who celebrated Easter personally with the Apostle John) and then bishop of Rome, Anicetus. It appeared that the churches in the east near the holy cities always celebrated Easter on the 14th of Nisan corresponding to the specific Old Testament Passover (*Leviticus 23:5*), independent on the day of the week. The church in Rome determined the Easter celebration should always fall specifically on a Sunday, the day Jesus rose from the dead. Polycarp kept the peace declaring it a difference of the days of celebration parting ways peacefully with Anicetus. The successor to the Roman church, Victor, was not as gracious as either Anicetus or Polycarp and declared all churches must abandon the 14th of Nisan fast and celebrate Easter as prescribed by the mother church in Rome. Victor thus determined every church who maintained the old date of celebration to be heretics and gave just cause for their persecution.

In 325, the Counsel of Nicaea dictated that Easter will always be celebrated on a Sunday and the date, though around the springtime, was merely determined by the

---

[i]The distinction between the lunar and solar calendar is significant because other holidays are connected with Saint's Days on specific days of the modern solar calendar, while Easter is roughly connected with the observance of the Jewish Passover which is always based on the Lunar calendar. The only other rotating holiday we celebrate is Thanksgiving and we will see that was set based on consumer trends, not religious pretense.

Roman church. This lead to several other controversies, discussions, and debates over the years which sought to clarify and calculate specific days to celebrate Easter. Some wanted to bind it to the Jewish Passover while others wanted to keep the date independently of the old calendar. In modern times, Easter is usually set as the first Sunday following the March equinox, though some calculations may alter that day slightly depending on whether the local church uses a Gregorian or a Julian calendar.

A council of churches sought to officially and perpetually assign Easter to the specific Sunday following the equinox as it generally occurs. This ratification would unify the two calendars and thus the churches of the world would have one joint day to celebrate Easter. The reforms were debated and agreed upon in 1997 with a 2001 adoption date, but the change in date has not yet occurred, so Easter remains on different dates for different churches around the world.

## THE PAGAN CONNECTION

Easter as a holiday may be the least influenced by Pagan traditions. Some elements of Easter, namely the bunny, baskets, and eggs, are not represented in the Bible, we also do not find evidence those were borrowed from any ancient cultures, but more likely they stemmed from medieval traditions. There is only one reference linking any Pagan practices to Easter but historians do not regard the connection as authoritative. A German monk named Bede lived between 673-735 and wrote about some supposed ancient customs. Bede, however, is known by historians to be biased and omissive in his writings meaning his version of history is not always accurate to his contemporaries. Regardless, he wrote in his piece translated *On The Reckoning of Time*:

> In olden times the English people—for it did not seem fitting that I should speak of other nations' observance of the year

and yet be silent about my own nation's—calculated their months according to the course of the Moon. Hence, after the manner of the Greeks and the Romans, [the months] take their name from the Moon, for the Moon is called mona and the month monath. The first month, which the Latins call January, is Giuli; February is called Solmonath; March Hrethmonath; April, Eosturmonath ... Eosturmonath has a name which is now translated "Paschal month" and which was once called after a goddess of theirs named Eostre, in whose honour feasts were celebrated in that month. Now they designate that Paschal season by her name, calling the joys of the new rite by the time-honoured name of the old observance.

The historians raise issue with the part about being named after a goddess called Eostre citing the term simply meant 'the beginning' referring to the springtime. Eostre is from the German tradition and is more often than not believed to be the name of the month of April before the calendar was changed to Paschal on the Christian calendar. Others have attested that Bede would keep paganism at a distance so he would not make up a goddess just to discredit it, but he also could have made up the goddess to explain ancient traditions surrounding equinoxes and seasons common in most primitive cultures. We do know from human history that humans are intrinsically religious and make up gods all the time (*Romans 1:21-23*). It is very possible Bede's writing is truthfully speculative, but both angles are mere speculation without additional historical writings which are sadly absent. With little other evidence of this goddess or a German ancestry connection, the pagan connections to Easter are shaky at best.

## EASTER THROUGH THE AGES

Easter was practiced by the disciples based on credible testimony from Polycarp about the worship of Easter on the 14th of Nisan. The traditions, dates, and practice of the holiday, however, morphed over time consistent with other holidays. In the Roman tradition, Easter marked the resurrection and thus the start of the new calendar year.

During the Nicene age of the church (311-590 AD) when other holidays were starting to emerge, Easter underwent metamorphosis. As symbolism became prominent in the church being spread from Rome, the season and practice of Lent was standardized as a forty day sacrifice symbolizing Jesus's wandering and temptation in the wilderness. This custom began as freewill offering in the spirit of giving outlined in *2 Corinthians 9:7*:

> *Each one must do just as he has purposed in his heart, not grudgingly or under compulsion, for God loves a cheerful giver.*

But eventually the practice became a mandate from church authorities.

Under Pope Gregory I whom fixed so many other festivals of the early church, the season of Lent was set to begin on Ash Wednesday when the people were to sprinkle themselves with dust and ashes to symbolize our dusty origins and final destiny (*Genesis 3:19*). Eventually this 40 day season, called Quadragesima, became known as a time of forgoing pleasure and indulgence. As such, weddings were soon forbidden and silence was demanded in both public and private life. The only allowable acts were those of charity and penance meaning the good intention quickly became an imposition of society and no longer a free will of the people.

The mandate to celebrate Easter on a church-appointed Sunday with the accompanying Lent requirements of Roman society led way for hypocrisy and legalism. The greatest example of hypocrisy was when St. Patrick's Day found its way onto the holiday calendar in the middle of Lent. The holiday generally focused on drinking and parties, both of which were forbidden in the solemn 40 days of Lent, so an exception of the Lent traditions were added to allow riotous living on Saint Patrick's Day. This is much like the transformation of many holidays into Christian cele-brations: the people would engage either way, so the church made it legal so as to quell a possible uprising.

The requirements around the many holidays including Easter became a commandment from the church rather than a willful time of dedication to the Savior. This created a ritual surrounding the sacrifice of Jesus Christ and thus became a means of disunity between the mother church in Rome and Swiss reformers. John Calvin, the chief teacher among the Swiss reformation in Geneva, was not in favor of keeping any holidays set by the church and he convinced the church to not participate. Eventually the Lutheran believers, whom held some jurisdiction in his territories, mandated by law to at least hold a service. As such, Calvin held services and preached, but he certainly had a disdain for any 'supposed' holy days the church in Rome had instituted.

The Lutheran protestants, however, kept the holiday which is why most of our Easter customs come from Germany, as they have been preserved, though in a purer form from the ritual present in the Roman church. The Lutherans held to the holiday mostly because they took a more objective approach to fixing the errors with the Roman church rather than merely dismissing their sacraments outright. In this case it is likely they held to the Easter tradition due to the writings about it from Polycarp and the early celebration of the holiday among the Anti-Nicene church fathers before corruption by the Roman Church.

## MODERN EASTER

In our modern age, Easter is bi-polar. The Dutch brought the holiday to this country but commercialism converted Easter into the secular helliday we know and love today. The post WWII industrial boom commercialized gifts, trinkets, and candy that has become the second most profitable holiday for confectioners behind Halloween. The secular world cares not for the resurrection Sunday and "He has risen indeed" is more scoffed than taken with pride in America today. Thus the secular holiday has grown into another commercial day for big box stores.

The other side to Easter remains in the churches. Whatever the denomination, most churches still hold the importance of Easter as Resurrection Sunday, the day Jesus Rose from the dead. Easter Sunday is one of the two days during the year many people show up to a church service, and so it has become a time to target non-believers with the Gospel. For some churches, it means they preach a clearer Gospel message, taking the call to evangelize seriously. Still other churches focus more on growth potential and ignore the difficult aspects of Scriptures favoring instead to cater to the desire for games and entertainment.

In any event, the two parts of Easter do merge in many churches as they preach the message of Jesus on Sunday morning, then provide Easter egg hunts for the children in the community. Easter has remained among the purest of holidays, and the inclusion of the cultural aspects like baskets and egg hunts should not be taken as pollution of the holiday so long as the church keeps a commitment to the Gospel in the main service. With that in mind, we will look at the origin of the cultural Easter elements, the bunny, the eggs, and the baskets, in this section.

## THE BUNNY

The modern Easter Bunny is a bit of an enigma. We know Pennsylvania Dutch settlers brought the rabbit to America around the 1700s but the Easter Bunny was adopted in Lutheran churches before that. The bunny was much like Santa Clause in that he would know which children were good and which ones were bad. The good boys and girls would get eggs, candy and toys delivered to them. The children would construct a nest for the bunny and often leave out carrots to eat. This was adapted into baskets we use to treat our children today.

As for the origin, it is hard to tell. Some have suggested the bunny was tied to a fertility cult of Eostre, a goddess of fertility, whose symbol was that of a rabbit indicating the frequency the animal's reproduction. However, these ideas were from Bede whom we already discussed as being non-authoritarian by experts in history.

As for the rabbit, many suggest the bunny was as a symbol of the Virgin Mary based on an old myth that rabbits are hermaphroditic, able to reproduce without losing their virginity. This would have been prominent for the Catholic faith which holds the belief that Mary remained a virgin for her entire life. All ancient cultures of antiquities celebrated spring, and birth was often acquainted with such times. This led to both the rabbits and the eggs being used to represent Easter.

Of course, like most other holidays, the Easter bunny in America is a cultural icon rather than a religious symbol. It is to be taken as a story and figure for children to enjoy the holiday and receive some gifts while we teach them why we celebrate the holiday and bestow it's meaning.

## THE EGG

Like the Easter Bunny, the Easter Egg has a somewhat mysterious origin. Some decry it as a pagan myth while others even suggest Christian myths going back to Mary Magdalene and the tomb. While the rabbit is an animal symbolizing the new growth in springtime, the egg is also a sign of fertility. The position of the egg is more complicated than the hare, however, because despite the egg always being a staple food item it was later forbidden to consume during Lent in the early days of the church. So as to not waste eggs, they were hard boiled for longer preservation. The eggs were later painted red to symbolize Christ's shed blood. On the Easter morning, Lent was officially over and the people were once again allowed to consume the eggs making them a staple food on Easter morning.

The German immigrants did not just bring the Easter Bunny to America, they also brought the eggs. The children would build a nest for the bunny which would come in the night to the good children and deliver eggs. The bunny would also bring toys, and the tradition evolved from there to include chocolates and candies. Once the consumer aspects of Easter caught on, the nests were replaced by baskets of straw and hidden. This gave rise to the children's game of searching for the Easter basket in the morning. Such games also included the eggs in the form of Easter Egg Hunts and Easter Egg Rolls which were downhill races of Easter Eggs by the children. The fascination with the Easter egg started with preserving them by hard boiling, rather than let them go to waste when they were a forbidden food during the prescribed Lent observations. The eggs provided cultural games to incorporate the eggs into discussions about the meaning of the holiday.

## BASKET

The history of the Easter Basket is even more mysterious than the rest of the holiday. The only thing agreed upon is the custom comes from Germany and is related to the legend of the Easter Hare. We know German Protestants included the legend of the Easter Hare in their traditional stories told to children. These stories were part of the Easter festivities as early as the 1600's but it is likely older in origins being related to the beginning of the German agricultural growing season. In the Protestant tradition, the Christian parents in Germany told their kids a hare would come and build an improvised nest from any objects available: straw, bonnets, or even baskets. The hare would lay eggs in the nests if the children were good during the year.

The tradition continued in Germany but was transplanted to the United States by Pennsylvania Dutch settlers. Once in America, the tradition caught on and the baskets were filled with eggs, toys, and candies before being hidden for children to hunt on Easter Sunday.

## THE CONSUMER SHIFT

In my eyes (Tyler), Easter has always been about consumerism so I'm not as mad with the holiday's consumer shift in our culture. This holy holiday had the same fate as the rest of the holidays: the real purpose has been squeezed out leaving only the gift-giving aspects. It's gotten so bad that many American families don't even know what Easter actually means: the wonderful occasion of Christ sacrificing Himself and rising from the dead to save us from our sins. Aside from not recognizing the Biblical application, everything in the way we celebrate the holiday today could be considered an extension, or even an evolution, of old-world Easter celebrations.

In America, Easter always involves a basket bursting with candy and gifts. This happened with the entrance into the Industrial Revolution allowing corporations to flood the market with inexpensive material products. Society teaches us that failure to buy Easter junk is akin to failing to love one's family. It appears this celebration is born of obligation, much like going to church, it's been in place so long we do not question it, and if we do not question it, we never change. The laws no longer mandate us to participate in the traditions, but entering any store in the Easter season means bombardment with adverts to fill the Easter baskets. Our giving may not be as genuine as we think if we need reminders to buy gifts to give. Such Easter spending seems more like an unspoken rule rather than a selfless act.

It is hard to say exactly when Easter became so corporate, but it was no doubt a slow process happening subtly over many decades starting with the Industrial

Revolution. A breakthrough and catalyst of this invasion, however, was the Great Depression. Corporate sprawl employing the masses was part of the reason we busted out of our economic turmoil, this was a way they gained influence and favor among the population. The roaring 50's and years leading up to it was the introduction of consumerism and we are feeling the effects today. We had undying blind obedience to marketing, and once the companies knew how much profit could be harvested from holidays, the hellidays were born and special days meant less about the gift giving and more about the obligation.

Easter is big business grossing about $823 million in 2015 according to Nielsen data. It earned its place snugly between Halloween and Christmas as the most economically profitable holidays, but it wasn't always so widely celebrated. The first American Easter celebrations arrived with the Dutch immigrants in the 1700's. German migrants brought rich traditions from old Germany which had a history in Easter celebrations. As the colonies increased trade with one another, not only products, but customs were traded. This spread German Easter traditions to other colonists. The influence of Easter spread slowly until the economic boom in the post-war 1950's.

Just recovering from the roaring 50's and still high on the wonder of color television and pride of their wealth, marketing became an American pastime in business. America was amassing riches and the economy stabilized. The survivors of the Great Depression saw their first sum of money in decades, so why not spend it? This became an imprint covering all future generations. "A lie becomes truth if told enough", is a quote credited to Vladimir Lenin and surely it is taken to heart by all of the marketing firms of "modern" times. This is the reason of our consumerist nature today. This very nature is what has forced not just Easter, but all major (and some minor) holidays into the center stage on their respective days.

## What The Church is Getting Right

Easter is one of the holidays the modern church usually gets right as a whole. The holiday has certainly changed over the years and much of the cultural additions, particularly the Easter Egg Hunts for children and the poinsettia flowers decorating the church, do not alter the general purpose of the day. Regardless, many people who are casually religious show up to church on Easter Sunday and churches traditionally preach on the death and resurrection of Jesus during the sermon. In fact, this is generally one of the few times many Western churches preach the Gospel at all!

The season usually starts a few weeks earlier in some churches or at least a week earlier in most. The modern consumer aspect ships in palm branches to wave at some point on the Sunday prior to Easter to commemorate, or in some cases reenact, the Triumphal Entry found in the synoptic Gospels:

*And many spread their coats in the road, and others spread leafy branches which they had cut from the fields. Those who went in front and those who followed were shouting:*

*"Hosanna!*
*Blessed is He who comes in the name of the Lord;*
*Blessed is the coming kingdom of our father David;*
*Hosanna in the highest!"*
*(Mark 11:8-10)*

The palm branches are passed out for the congregation to wave or for some members to enter the church singing Hosanna to the Highest. This Sunday the week before Easter is often used to talk about what Jesus came to do.

The following Sunday, Easter, which is one of the Sundays many unchurched people make their presence known, usually to accommodate family, the churches often focus on what is called The Passion of the Christ, though not to be confused with the movie bearing that title. The Passion is the crucifixion and subsequent resurrection from the dead to save the world from their sins. This is the Gospel preached on Easter morning and this is the true mission of the church. For these reasons, we believe the modern Easter services are one of the purest holidays still gracing the Western world in the church.

To conclude our chapter on Easter, we believe that while not pure, this holiday is an example for how the church should respond to all holidays. They use their position to tell the real story and then preach the Gospel of Jesus Christ. People who attend church on this day will generally hear about how Jesus came to the earth, was perfect in all ways, and died on the cross for their sins by His own choice. While the holiday does still include many consumer aspects, it is one the church has not raised the white flag of surrender to, and for that, we should look to Easter as an example of how a church should reach the community.

# Happy Helloween

## TOM'S REFLECTION ON HALLOWEEN

Like most kids, our growing up revolved around two perfect holidays. Obviously Christmas was the first, but what else could possibly rival Halloween? In those days, we were allowed to roam the streets after dark mostly unsupervised. We adorned costumes of all kinds and ran from house to house seeking the Holy Grail of all junk food. Our endeavors finally resulted in bags of amazing candies, well, all except the pixie sticks (My mother would always throw those away and I confess I never ate a pixie stick until I was an adult). Halloween was rife with parties at school, after school, in the neighborhood, and I usually even went Trick or Treating twice because I had a friend in a neighboring city which always seemed to celebrate Halloween on a different day from our town. This was not a day of evil or witches or devils, but rather it was a day of junk-food-topia to indulge the beginning of the school year until the Christmas celebrations. Yes, beside the coveted 10 days off of school over Christmas break, Halloween was the best of holidays.

### TYLER'S REFLECTION ON HALLOWEEN

For me, Halloween has always been about one thing: candy. All us kids looked forward to the treats at our early Halloween festival in my church parking lot. Our church held a Halloween fair every year, that gave us lots of candy from familiar faces with very little walking. It was a good event, very relaxed, but looking back, I did not feel God's presence at the event. It borrowed nearly everything from the culture, a carbon-copy of Halloween parties at friends houses, in school, but this one just happened to be at the church. It was not specifically Godly, but neither was it bad. They were good times in any event because our reward, the candy, was easy obtained.

## THE ROOTS OF EVIL

A simple internet search for Halloween provides a variety of histories, opinions, and views on the origin and purpose of this holiday. For Christians, bookstores and various Christian websites administer weapons to get armed for battle with the devils of Halloween. Is it really such a horrible helliday celebrated by witches and Satanists or is there more to this day than meets the eye? This chapter will discuss the history of the holiday without the biases often accompanying other Christian material on the subject. Our discussion will take us into the consumer culture surrounding this day. We will then discuss the ways the church has responded to the holiday over the years, and finally we will talk about methods the church can use to positively respond to the day most attributed to demons, witches, and devils.

Many histories boldly declare that Halloween started as a celebration of Samhain (pronounced SOW-ween), the Celtic (or druid) god of death. According to these sources, the Druids believed in reincarnation and worshiping the false god would save loved ones from being reincarnated into some lesser life form. We discount this as an origin to the modern day Halloween festivities because the Druid culture overwhelmingly did not keep written records. The pieces of information from varied conquerors and archaeologists is all we have to describe such cultures, and that lends to very biased information. We also point out even Ankerbergs book gets most of the Druid conversation from Encyclopedia Brittanica Macropedia. If one were to discount a holiday from a Christian perspective, human sacrifice attributed to Druids worshiping the god of death is definitely a great angle!

As for verifiable information on the origins of Halloween, the name actually has Christian roots. In 607 Bishop of Rome Bontiface IV dedicated the Pantheon to "the service of God in the name of the ever-Virgin Mary and all martyrs[i]". The commemoration became known as All Saints Day, which the eastern church was already celebrating around Pentecost. It is unclear exactly when the date was transferred to November 1st, but in 835, Gregory the IV standardized All Saints Day to be celebrated empire-wide on November 1st while the related holiday, All Souls Day, was celebrated on November 2nd. The term Halloween comes from the night before All Saints Day, which was a holy day, or in that time period, a Hallow Day. So the night before All Saints Day became known as All Hallows Eve, eventually shortened to Hallow eve or Halloween.

As the years progressed, the holiday became a day spent praying people out of purgatory in the Catholic tradition. The purgatory angle became the initial cause for protestant disdain for this day in the Catholic calendar, and consequently in 1517 at midnight on Halloween Martin Luther nailed his 95 theses to the door of the church in Wittenberg to discuss the matter of indulgences. This was standard practice to initiate public debate over the issues he observed in the ruling church of the day. The close relationship between Halloween and the Catholic All Saints

---

[i]The History of the Christian Church, Volume 4: Medieval Christianity, Section 99, Philip Schaff

Day (to venerate many saints) precipitated the banishing of the holiday from reformation and puritan communities. The puritans biased everything against Catholic traditions, and in desire to set up a state religion in America modeling it after Calvin's state of church in Geneva, they banned Halloween. As such, Halloween was not celebrated in the United States until the mid 1800s when immigrants brought the modern version of Halloween to America.

## RAISING THE DEAD

Our modern Halloween festivities actually come from a cross between Celtic customs and the Irish Catholic All Saints Evening which was brought to us from Irish migrants during the potato famine immigration to the United States. We have some detail about the old-Irish celebrations from the *Book of Days*. Even the author of that book says it:

> Is clearly a relic of pagan times, for there is nothing in the church-observance of the ensuing day of All Saints to have originated such extraordinary notions as are connected with, this celebrated festival, or such remarkable practices as those by which it is distinguished.

The holiday was often celebrated with apples and nuts. The traditional 'bobbing for apples' (called Ducking for Apples in that day) was actually a game at Halloween parties for the younger kids, but the older kids had some more romantic games. One custom named nuts after lovers and if the owners nut burned in fire with another they were destined to be married. Still another party game was to be blindfolded and led to three bowls. The blindfolded participant would dip their hand into one of three bowls, indicting the marriage of a maiden, widow, or to remain unmarried. Another game the youths would pull up a stalk of colewort from the garden and the size of the bulb corresponded to whom they may marry or what their life fortune may be.

Other English and Irish references point to costumes and going house to house collecting toys or candies. The root of costumes probably lay in the Catholic traditions. Accordingly since All Saint's Day was a popular Catholic holiday the demons and spirits were said to roam the earth the day before tempting people. The people wore disguises so the spirits did not recognize them. Thus out of the veneration of the saints on November 1$^{st}$ was born the tradition of wearing a costume on October 31$^{st}$ to avoid being targeted by demons. This tradition of costumes and candy came to the United States.

The games and costumes are not the only part of our modern Halloween derived from Irish culture. Even the popular Jack o' Lantern seems to come partially from an Irish legend (many other ancient peoples told the story, but our modern implementation is specifically Irish). Stingy Jack, as he was called, tricked the Devil in a series of schemes. He convinced the Devil to become a coin to pay the bill for drinks, but Jack ran off without paying, keeping the Devil in that form with a crucifix in his pocket. He again tricked the Devil into never claiming his soul, but for his deeds he also forfeited his way into heaven so he was destined to roam the earth with only a charcoal ember to light his way. Jack carved a lantern from a gourd and placed the ember in it as a lamp. The Irish would thus use the Jack 'o Lantern as a good luck charm to ward off the evil spirits. While the Irish used turnips, beets, and potatoes, the customary pumpkin occurred when they arrived in America to find pumpkins were larger and easier to carve than the produce from their old country.

This legend, however, does not explain the Halloween tradition though many use this story as the explanation for our carved pumpkin décor. The reality is, the legend of Stingy Jack was told to explain the natural phenomena of the Will o' the Wisp, which is igniting swamp gas. Nevertheless, the carved lanterns did not make an appearance in the New World until after the great Irish immigration around 1847. After that point, it was first used in autumn pranks by kids to cause mischief. Eventually, pumpkin carving became known from appearances in newspaper articles as crafts for kids. It would appear the first instance of the Jack o' Lantern being used in Halloween was in 1892. Atlanta, Georgia Mayor Hemphill and his wife threw an elaborate Halloween party including carved pumpkins as the décor. The local newspaper the following day ran articles about the elaborately decorated party including the popular Jack o' Lanterns and since then, the carved pumpkin has been a mark of Halloween.

## But is it Evil?

The relationship between Halloween and Wicca or Halloween and Satanism is shakier than the rest of the Halloween traditions. As mentioned above, the reason Halloween was not practiced in America prior to the Irish Immigration lay exclusively in that it was connected to a Catholic holiday but the puritans laid most of the Christian foundation in the New World specifically rejecting Catholic traditions. But we want to take some time to dispel myths about this helliday and modern pagan practice. First, we will address the issue of Witchcraft and Satan worship.

There have been people who discount Halloween as evil citing Satan is even evoked for his power on Halloween more than any other night. John MacArthur correctly commented that Satan is not any more active on Halloween than he is on other days. Even according to self-professed (and actually studied) Satanists, Halloween is a day enjoyed by them, but not one of any particular importance. The day considered the most important to the Satanist is actually their own birthday because Satanism is at its root the worship of oneself. Witchcraft, being more of an ancient and pagan holiday does in fact celebrate Halloween as a holy day for them for reasons mentioned above regarding harvests, end of growing seasons, and the change of seasons.

But does that make Halloween specifically Wiccan? Not any more than Christmas is Jewish because they celebrate Hanukkah at nearly the same time. So here is the bottom line: If Halloween for you is Wicca, than it is Wicca, if it is a day to pray souls out of purgatory, than that is what it is, if it is a day to dress up in a costume and get free candy, than that is what Halloween is for you. For the purposes of this book, we focus on the way western consumerism has sucked all elements of holiness from any religious days and replaced it with the idol of materialism as evidenced by the appearance of the Halloween sales before the back to school sales have run their course.

## MASKED IN CONSUMERISM

The idea of Halloween costumes is nothing new. The origins of the costumes have been convoluted throughout history and it only gets more confusing as you delve deeper down the rabbit hole of theories regarding the creation of this tradition. One of the most acceptable origins for Halloween costumes is the pagan festivals utilizing them. The pagans would wear masks to ward off, attract, or absorb the spirits of the night. If they were aiming to absorb a specific spirit, say a horse or a skeleton, they would wear a horse or skeleton costume to presumably trick the spirits. Arguably, costumes have gotten more "of-the-culture" during the Renaissance Period; with the rejuvenation of art, fashion, and literature, the focus on the costumes had inherently gotten more artsy. It didn't get much better when the Edwardian Era influenced fashion allowing corsets and bustles to become the new goal for women, potentially giving birth to the idea we've had ever since.

The costumes of today have completely abandoned the original tradition of hiding from demons. We now opt for dressing up as our favorite pop culture figures from movies, music, television shows, and social media. Consumerism has long since taken over the costume market and has since mastered the art of appealing to our desires, good or bad, and we keep going deeper down the rabbit hole of celebrity idol worship. It has gotten us trapped in a loop. Consumerism isn't the only thing that has us beat; a potentially bigger and badder opponent is in our midst: sexuality.

There is a fascinating correlation between the current corruptness of the culture and the Halloween costumes. As the collective sexual thirst of our society increases, so does the skimpiness of the costumes people wear on Halloween. Girls have always been seen as the fashion pushers of each era, they seem to have the power to change what's 'in' and 'out' about the scope of fashion, and in a strange way, they can control certain aspects of guy's whims. Men from crumbling civilizations throughout history have focused on sexual aspects of women. When you combine a longing of these women wanting to be "accepted" by corrupt men, these corrupt men being a mass populous of our current society, and these women setting these fashion trends, it's a recipe for absolute disaster. We are not single handedly blaming women, men, or society on this, but we're giving each of the groups a slice of the blame pie because it's a continuous cycle and each group is the hamster on this wheel at one point. Sexual Halloween costumes are just one adverse side effect of a culture too obsessed with sex and though you think it might not be that big of a deal, this could turn into a nasty ripple effect. This is why we need to stop this now. Actions that are acted in the present always have some predecessor in the future and who knows what this could spawn. We really are in deep waters in the moment and no man power is going to get us out of this rut. The only way to get out of this mess is to have a real mass conversion to Christ, and we don't know how likely that is.

## CHRISTIAN HALLOWEEN FESTIVALS

While some people denounce Halloween as a day to worship Satan, others want to capitalize on the publicity. We see three general responses to Halloween specific to the Christian community. On Halloween in Wyoming where Tom lived for several years, businesses in the old part of town opened up in the afternoon to hand out candy to costumed kids. It was fascinating to see how the various churches downtown responded to the celebrations surrounding them. One church celebrated by dressing in Bible costumes and handing out healthy snacks and Bible tracts while other members of the congregation walked through the crowds engaging people in conversations. Contrary to that, many churches downtown simply closed their doors not wanting to participate in the festivities. One church, however, set up a freaky haunted house. I wanted to know what this house of God was doing for the day so I paid the two dollars to walk through the madhouse. Fake blood was splashed through the church as if it were a murder scene, and the same ghosts and goblins meandered the corridors as if lost from the secular displays in the rest of the community. This church adopted the full cultural mindset of day.

We see from just the churches in our sample community three responses, so is it worthy of determining if there is a correct or incorrect response from the church. We do not want to judge churches but rather goad them into a direction consistent with the Christian mission. We considered the mission of the church in The Bunny and the Tomb, so here we will consider our response to the world.

## SALT AND LIGHT

We already looked at the Scriptures about being salt and light, but it is worth repeating here. In the Sermon on the Mount, Jesus tells us to be salt and light to the world:

> *You are the salt of the earth; but if the salt has become tasteless, how can it be made salty again? It is no longer good for anything, except to be thrown out and trampled under foot by men.*
>
> *You are the light of the world. A city set on a hill cannot be hidden; nor does anyone light a lamp and put it under a basket, but on the lampstand, and it gives light to all who are in the house. Let your light shine before men in such a way that they may see your good works, and glorify your Father who is in heaven (Matthew 6:13-16).*

This gives us two solid analogies for how Christians are to conduct themselves in the world. Salt is a preservative able to prevent meat from going rancid. This increases the shelf life making salt a critical staple of the ancient middle east. Such a preservative is needed to prevent our culture from going wicked. One role Christians should have in this world is to prevent the evil bound in the heart of every man to impose its destruction on the world. As salt, Christians are to help God in preventing the world from falling into pure chaos.

Light is a guiding path, as the Psalmist also says in *Psalm 119:105*:

> *Your word is a lamp to my feet*
> *And a light to my path.*

Christians have the Word to direct our decisions, but the world has no such guidance; it is up to believers in any generation to illuminate a righteous walk in this present world. As we live in the Word we learn the way to God, and as we live in the world we are to take that light to a dark culture.

Taken together, Christians are supposed to prevent the culture from sliding further into their generational sin while showing people the way to Jesus. We have further personal callings in specific ministries, but those all fall into either preservation of the world or administrating the

Gospel. Paul exhorts us in *Ephesians 4:17* to *walk no longer as the Gentiles walk.*

The "haunted" church adopted the cultural practices and set up a haunted house with every symbol called evil by the conservative congregations. There was no Gospel, no separation from the culture, just pure immersion into the secular practices surrounding them in the world. Without any outreach, the people demonstrated the church to be in the world, but also of the world. While I agree this was the most non-threatening approach the church could take, it is not the place of the church to conform to the world. Consider *Romans 12:2:*

> *Do not be conformed to this world, but be transformed by the renewing of your mind, so that you may prove what the will of God is, that which is good and acceptable and perfect.*

While the context of this verse is a more personal application, we can understand the overarching principle that believers should not conform to the practices of the world, and this means taking the cultural cues from the festivities around them whether satanic or otherwise. In failing to prevent cultural displays from imitating the world and failing to show a way to Christ, we reject the third church's approach to the Halloween festivals.

While this church was active in the seasonal festivities, it was not activity consistent with the calling Christ makes on His people or His church. People in the community might have learned this church's name after the haunted house, but it was not for being a place of holy worship. The involvement in such an activity showed participation in the evil elements which can be present in Halloween rather than focusing on the more benign traditions in the American holiday. This church did not demonstrate salt, preserving the culture, nor did it demonstrate light – the showing of the way to Christ. It instead conformed itself to the mores of the day walking back into the Gentile world Paul repeatedly admonishes us to avoid.

## In The World But Not Of The World

Next is the congregation who participated with Bible costumes, tracts, and healthier snacks. This church was in the community, participating, but doing so appropriately. They realized the day was not merely a Wicca or satanic day of celebration but something adopted into the culture of our society. While Christians are to be in the world but not of the world, we do not have the command to completely isolate ourselves from the festivities accepted by the state. As long as sin is not required for involvement in said activities.

While a haunted house is certainly one of the many aspects of Halloween, it is also arguable that harvest, costumes, candy, and the like are equally important cultural icons of the day. The church who dressed in pleasant costumes were participating in the local holiday without hypocrisy. As such, they did not contribute to the decay by dressing as vile creatures or witches. They helped show people they could enjoy the day without succumbing to the evil elements.

Regarding light, this church handed out tracts and information about their church and salvation. While we are not generally people who care much for the Bible tracts, we think a holiday like this is one of the places they merit an appearance. This is a day people go door to door asking for something from the house. In this case people were knocking on God's house and the congregation answered with a booklet about Jesus Christ, the greatest light of all!

This church remembered our calling as Christians is to preach the Gospel:

*How then will they call on Him in whom they have not believed? How will they believe in Him whom they have not heard? And how will they hear without a preacher? How will they preach unless they are sent? Just as it is written, "HOW BEAUTIFUL ARE THE FEET OF THOSE WHO BRING GOOD NEWS OF GOOD THINGS!" (Romans 10:14-15)*

As such, they used the daily activities to fulfill the Great Commission and demonstrated a church can participate in Halloween without embracing the darker elements. In short, they preserved the culture by showing a harvest type display devoid of evil images. We believe this church was most in the right.

## HOLIER THAN THOU ART

The last church ignored the echoes of the children outside choosing to remain closed. Depending on the church leaders, this could be a valid response to Halloween because we are commanded to follow our conscience on matters not directly set forth in the Scriptures. *1 Corinthians 8* discusses gray area decisions well:

*Concerning the eating of things sacrificed to idols, we know that there is no such thing as an idol in the world, and that there is no God but one. For even if there are so-called gods whether in heaven or on earth, as indeed there are many gods and many lords, yet for us there is but one God, the Father, from whom are all things and we exist for Him; and one Lord, Jesus Christ, by whom are all things, and we exist through Him. However not all men have this knowledge; but some, being accustomed to the idol until now, eat food as if it were sacrificed to an idol; and their conscience being weak is defiled. But food will not commend us to God; we are neither the worse if we do not eat, nor the better if we do eat. But take care that this liberty of yours does not somehow become a stumbling block to the weak. For if someone sees you, who have knowledge, dining in an idol's temple, will not his conscience, if he is weak, be strengthened to eat things sacrificed to idols? For through your knowledge he who is weak is ruined, the brother for whose sake Christ died. And so, by sinning against the brethren and wounding their conscience when it is weak, you sin against Christer. Therefore, if food causes my brother to stumble, I will never eat meat again, so that I will not cause my brother to stumble (1 Corinthians 8:4-13).*

This passage deals specifically with food offered to idols – a capital offense in the Old Testament law, but a common practice in the city of Corinth to whom the original letter was addressed. It is not out of context to apply this to any controversial gray-area decision where some believers say to partake but others denounce the activity as 'From the Devil!' Due to the polarizing opinions of Halloween in modern Christian circles, this is the best holiday for this point to be elaborated.

To explain gray-area decisions, we first need to know something about the direct commands in the Bible. In the early church when the Gentiles started becoming Christians, the Jewish believers in their towns were claiming the Greeks needed to follow the Mosaic law, so Paul takes the question back to the Apostles and we find this discussion:

*The apostles and the elders came together to look into this matter. After there had been much debate, Peter stood up and said to them, "Brethren, you know that in the early days God made a choice among you, that by my mouth the Gentiles would hear the word of the gospel and believe. And God, who knows the heart, testified to them giving them the Holy Spirit, just as He also did to us; and He made no distinction between us and them, cleansing their hearts by faith. Now therefore why do you put God to the test by placing upon the neck of the disciples a yoke which neither our fathers nor we have been able to bear? But we believe that we are saved through the grace of the Lord Jesus, in the same way as they also are. (Acts 15:6-11)"*

### And the Apostles replied with a letter:

*The apostles and the brethren who are elders, to the brethren in Antioch and Syria and Cilicia who are from the Gentiles, greetings. Since we have heard that some of our number to whom we gave no instruction have disturbed you with their words, unsettling your souls, it seemed good to us, having become of one mind, to select men to send to you with our beloved Barnabas and Paul, men who have risked their lives for the name of our Lord Jesus Christ. "Therefore we have sent Judas and Silas, who themselves will also report the same things by word of mouth. "For it seemed good to the Holy Spirit and to us to lay upon you no greater burden than these essentials: that you abstain from things sacrificed to idols and from blood and from things strangled and from fornication; if you keep yourselves free from such things, you will do well. Farewell. (Acts 15:23-29)*

We see the Greek world was not commanded to directly adopt the Jewish laws, but we also need to recognize this answer is not complete because they did not have the full New Testament cannon including several other directives from the apostles. We can find from the Fruit of the Flesh in *Galatians 5* and the other writings from Paul where he gives us moral directives. For example, Paul encourages us to walk in a manner worthy of being called followers of Jesus and not like the rest of the world:

*So this I say, and affirm together with the Lord, that you walk no longer just as the Gentiles also walk, in the futility of their mind, being darkened in their understanding, excluded from the life of God because of the ignorance that is in them, because of the hardness of their heart; and they, having become callous, have given themselves over to sensuality for the practice of every kind of impurity with greediness (Ephesians 4:17-19).*

Paul makes other proclamations about sin to avoid in *1 Corinthians 6:18* when he says":

*Flee immorality. Every other sin that a man commits is outside the body, but the immoral man sins against his own body.*

We need to spend some time in the Bible learning about the commands New Testament believers are held to account for, and what is open to believers as their conscience allows.

With this consideration, anything the Bible does not specifically speak against is not directly forbidden in the life of the Christian. Applying this principle to Halloween, while the Bible does forbid witchcraft, Halloween is clearly not a holiday to participate in such religions even though some of the imagery of the holiday is directly consumer-focused images of fan-fiction witches. The core of the helliday is sadly selling costumes, candy, and classic Halloween propaganda. For the person who looks at Halloween and sees only evil, avoiding the holiday is the best choice because your conscience is bothered, but forcing other's into your view is sin (with the obvious exception that parents are permitted to make such distinctions for their young children).

Taken together, while the church is not commanded to avoid Halloween, if the majority of the church members see more evil in the day than good, it is best for that church to close their doors for the day, but they should not be critical of the churches who make an appropriate response to the holiday.

We as believers should take these expressions onto ourselves. We are free to take part in Halloween, but we should always seek to honor Christ in what we do, so make sure our celebrations bring honor to God and reflect our commitment to Jesus.

When it is all boiled down, Halloween in America is an American holiday, devoid of devotion and God. If we use it as a way to have clean fun, there is no reason to condemn it as evil. We definitely see some concerning roots in Halloween, and we do believe some people go way too far down the wrong path. Just this year, we heard about very small children dressing as 'hookers', people who forget children are scared of lunatics with chainsaws running around, and some people dress as sexually provocative or downright sick and evil things. Pagans will be pagans, and if you are a pagan reading this, I would ask you to simply remember that other people will see you; keep decency in the public parts of our world at large. But for the Christian, called to a higher standard, do not engage in the evil elements of the day, but have good clean fun, and remember to whom you belong. You do not want to ruin your Christian testimony for a party even if your intent is simply enjoyment.

Furthermore, when we consider Halloween as an American holiday, it has very little to do with witches or the Devil. The real focus is to sell orange and black merchandise with images of ghosts and goblins. It is a season to peer-pressure the culture into buying decorations and candy, while decking out the house as the set for the latest horror flick. If there is anything to avoid in the Halloween season, it is to be aware of the dangers in consumerism that may set us on spending money we should wisely place into other plans and investments rather than enrich the lives of companies selling cheap plastic trinkets.

# Gobbled Up by Consumerism

## TOM ON GIVING THANKS

Thanksgiving was always a weird holiday for me. Looking through my memories I cannot recall a single time I celebrated the day with my nuclear family, though I am sure there must have been at least one. I usually ended up at my aunt and uncles house, mostly because we were not a well off family and my mother would get paid extra for working holidays, so she usually worked Thanksgiving. The day itself holds fond memories of Chicken in a Biscuit crackers, black olives, and pickles. We had good times with my cousin over the holiday, but like many holidays for my dysfunctional family, the day also held many common relational challenges, and more hard conversations than fond memories. Maybe it is a good thing I do not remember a lot of Thanksgivings.

## TYLER'S ON GIVING THANKS

Thanksgiving in my opinion is the best holiday. Despite my Thanksgivings usually turning out like National Lampoons Christmas Vacation portraying crazy uncles, OCD grandmas, and that annoying cousin that gets away with everything, in my eyes, it's the least torched by bad American consumerism. In the days leading up to Thanksgiving, I'm less thinking "What am I getting this year?" like Christmas or "How many people will be over?" like New Years, I'm more thinking "What has my family been up to?" There's no 'target turkey' you have to get, in fact, it's even become socially acceptable to bring a ham instead, by no means a perfect holiday, but it's the closest we have to our country's true roots.


## THE LOST HOLIDAY

Thanksgiving is the lost holiday. It is the only truly American faith-based holiday, after all. It was founded when our ancestors left ties with their own countries to mix together in the New World experiment. Regardless, Thanksgiving is the only real celebrated religious federal holiday we have which is not tied to any ancient religious festival or celebrations. We say it is lost because it is neatly tucked between the two kid days: Halloween and Christmas. The former as a social day requiring candy, costumes, and provides a break from the back-to-school rush. The latter is the day which Ralphie calls the day which "*the day around which the kid calendar revolves*" in the famous movie *A Christmas Story*.

We have observed the changing corner colors of the Western stores throughout this book, but have you ever noticed there are no colors or catchy little trinkets associated with Thanksgiving? There are only two clear markings of the start of Thanksgiving: The proliferation of Pumpkin Spice[i]...everything and the local grocer skimping out the meat department to make room for the flock of frozen turkeys. Let us not also forget the United States President takes up his most serious official duty of pardoning a turkey every Thanksgiving. Otherwise,

---

[i]Pumpkin Spice is the seasonal cousin of unknown origin arriving, but not connected to any holiday in particular.

Thanksgiving is merely a day to catch the football games and the famous Macy's Day Parade. And let us not forget Black Friday. In fact, as of 2015, Thanksgiving is merely the second of a three day 'special day' sequence. Blackout Wednesday is a day of American drinking (maybe getting prepped up for the day spent awkwardly with family). Then we have Thanksgiving to watch parades and Football, and all that gears up for Black Friday to run out in masses in search of the coveted holiday sales so we can be sure to get great deals on all the junk we buy for Christmas.

Christmas overtakes Thanksgiving every year. Before the Halloween rush is over, the witches and demons must share shelf space with the angels, stars, crosses, and imagery of religious sentiment and of course, Santa. It is as if the evil is overtaken by the good as the orange and black shelves become clothed in white as if foreshadowing the angelic victory in Armageddon. But in reality it is not about the salvation offered by Christ, but big business making a lot of money on the masses who buy into Black Friday sales and fall to peer pressure of buying excessive things for every person in their life. As one friend of ours once said, "We should just stand in a circle, reach into our wallets for a $20 bill and pass it to the guy to the right". This sums up the helliday as we have forgotten what to be thankful for while we look to the shopping centers and advertising to discover what will fulfill our angst.

In all, Thanksgiving is just a stepping stone into the end of the year. It does not have a long-term root of faith, but rather many little offshoots, all relating to God. And as our culture becomes more hostile to God every year it is no wonder Thanksgiving has lost its way. Many people would be happy to see the day vanish all together, while others see it as a day of gluttony.

The official date itself has less to do with giving thanks than it does being related to consumer industry! It was traditionally the last Thursday of November, but every few years there are five Thursdays in the month and many retail stores considered that too late to start the Christmas sales season...significant because there was a time it was considered anathema to put up our Christmas decorations before Thanksgiving was over. The business owners won the debate and Franklin D Roosevelt thus declared the fourth Thursday was the official day to celebrate Thanksgiving. That means there is always one more Saturday in November, thus was born the original start of the Christmas shopping season. So we see even the date of celebration cannot escape the pull of consumerism!

## And Some Would be Thankful to See it Go

Certain groups have started making a big deal about the origin of Thanksgiving saying we are celebrating the murder of the Indians[i] and the theft of their land. Sadly the issue is more complicated than to brush it off without examination. There was a feast, in fact a few of them around 1621. One of the first feasts called the First Thanksgiving was a three day celebration between the Pilgrams and the Indians. The Pilgrims landed on Plymouth Rock in December and if it was not for the help of the natives, they would likely have all perished, but with their support, the Pilgrims thrived. The following season led to a plentiful harvest and they shared a long feast with the tribe who helped them survive.

Other accounts, however, hold traditional Days of Thanksgiving as early as 1607 in Virginia. But while the Indian relations in the northeast were generally peaceful, warring factions were breaking out in the more southern Virginia region and in March of 1622 the Indians massacred

---

[i] We chose to use "Indians" instead of "Native Americans" to keep in the culture with which the Holiday was founded. Tom grew up without anyone being offended by "Indians" and they even said "Indian Style" when asking kids to sit down in class. Tyler grew up as a Millennial in the "Safe Space" bubble and was told it was mean to call them "Indians" and they sat Criss Cross Apple Sauce and to Tom that sounds like playing Tic-Tac-Toe in your apple sauce, and one should never play with his food.

about two thirds of the Colonial settlements as the natives in these parts believed the white man merely wanted to kill the Indians to steal their land. To them, war was inevitable.

Taken together, while the settlers did war with the natives, the natives warred just as much. Sad as it is, war was the way of life back then. Being taken together, the modern Native American tribes are not completely against the Thanksgiving holiday because it was not specifically about the arrival of the white settlers, it was more about giving thanks to a higher power.

## A YOUNG MAN'S PERSPECTIVE

Thanksgiving is the holy pinnacle of the modern holidays, at least it's the best we've got in comparison to the rest of the holidays we're covering in this book. Seemingly untouched by the consumerism that plagues the lot of them, it's easily the most rooted in its classic ways and doesn't even stray too far from the original celebration. This holiday has gotten a bad rap as potentially supporting the settlers who engaged in conquest and war, but keep in mind that the Indians were also involved in slaughtering the colonists.

I (Tyler) recall times at thanksgiving dinners when we would go around the table and say something we're thankful for while we eat our turkey. We were all generic, saying things like God or family, but it's some tradition that remains long standing.

Turkey sales plummeted a estimated $69.9 million[i]. This is partly due to the increase of animal awareness and vegan folk but you can't deny the surprisingly large devaluation of turkey, maybe something more is at play. We've discussed a a lot about consumerism aspects of these holidays, however, there is a far more innocent way a holiday loses its relevancy, a need for change. I'm not in

---

[i]Turkey Sales Plummet as Vegan Thanksgiving Options Expand, *Compassion Over Killing*, November 15, 2018

support or against saving the animals, but it could be important to this new world we're adapting to, searching for alternatives to turkey or ham to save a life. The websites saying the celebration is going downhill may be missing the black swan in their data analysis: the main course substitute. Ham and tofu turkeys are sometimes replacing the traditional bird, and they're becoming more popular as the years go on. I'm not much of a stickler for the food you're eating, more of how you handle the holiday as a whole.

To address the Indian's relevance to the holiday from their perspective, should we celebrate it? Do they celebrate it? Is it respectful for them to celebrate it? The answer the modern society wants us to say is no to all of these, but we have to dive into history to get the full scope of this question. A good place to begin is the American Indian relationship. The schools teach us it was universal that Americans did not like the Indians and actively tried to kick them out but that's not completely true. As explained in this chapter, the dynamic was different all around the states with the north having great communication and the south being the more generalized view. These southern states are where the horror stories of war and borderline genocide took place, due to the harsher winters up north the need for survival and diplomacy was needed, that's our theory of the schism in treatment. What does this have to do with Thanksgiving? The depiction of the holiday we most commonly see in schools is of the diplomatic north while our overall generalization stems from the... barbaric south, how confusing.

What do the Indians think of Thanksgiving in this new age? It's all across the board, but believe it or not the ideas that originated centuries ago still exist in the soul of Indians. Keeler, who's a Dineh Nation representative (and oddly from the North tribes) celebrates Thanksgiving because she views her survival with gratefulness. She also carries on the tradition of helping others. She states that the Indians have suffered all of these tragedies and still continue to help. Keeler has to celebrate and commemorate her ancestors. Sherman Alexie, who hails from the Spokane tribe states a similar thing, saying that they have the most broken hearted guests and simply want to comfort in the same manner her ancestors did. There are Indians on the other end of the thought spectrum, mostly tribes that warred with the Americans, let's take Tavares Avant, who's a representative of the Wampanoag tribe located in Massachusetts. He believes that thanksgiving was celebrated out of a "conquest" and taking over of their land.

A lot of controversy surrounds thanksgiving and with this growing social justice movement and Indian press about the holiday, I don't see it slowing anytime in the near future. There's a lot of information online that supports any type of argument, it's hard to navigate what the 'right' answer is and the fire of 'is it okay to celebrate this?' will never fully be put out, but one thing is certain, it is the most rooted whether you like it or not.

## WHAT STARTED IT ALL

Thanksgiving as a holiday does not have a specific origin as simple as Pilgrims and Indians coming together for a big turkey dinner. It is true the natives helped the Pilgrims survive their first winter and the Pilgrims reciprocated the generosity during the bountiful harvest of 1621 with a feast. While these mostly peaceful celebrations were happening in the Massachusetts colonies, war with the Indians was threatening the population of the settlers in Virginia, even causing the colonists to band together into larger cities for defenses. Even in these colonies, the people did still get together at least one time in the year for a day of thanksgiving to God.

The first known feast of thanksgiving was not even in 1621, but 1607, but this date has fallen out of favor in that the original colony was soon after abandoned. This 1607 feast also did not include the Indians, but rather was a celebration to God for good tidings, not unlike most of the congressional appointed Thanksgivings in America.

Thanksgiving was specifically a Christian or least a deist celebration. The 1621 feast in Plymouth was dedicated to the Christian God, giving thanks to Him for their bountiful harvest. The colonists who celebrated the feast were either Separatists or Puritans. Both of these groups were very dedicated to protestant Christianity, both being Calvinist reformers. The difference lay in that the Puritans wanted to clean up the corruption in the Church of England while maintaining their allegiance, but the Separatists wanted to proclaim independence from the church. Both were dedicated specifically to the Christian God and the Thanksgiving Proclamations were an extension of their faith.

As the country lay in birth-pains of war, several days of thanks were proclaimed sometimes more than once per year, and not generally following the pattern of a November harvest. Even on the national level, Thanksgiving was proclaimed a holiday of faith. The first congressional adoption called for national thanks began:

> For as much as it is the indispensable Duty of all Men to adore the superintending Providence of Almighty God; to acknowledge with Gratitude their Obligation to him for Benefits received, and to implore such farther Blessings as they stand in Need of: And it having pleased him in his abundant Mercy, not only to continue to us the innumerable Bounties of his common Providence; but also to smile upon us in the Prosecution of a just and necessary War, for the Defense and Establishment of our unalienable Rights and Liberties; particularly in that he hath been pleased, in so great a Measure, to prosper the Means used for the Support of our Troops, and to crown our Arms with most signal success[i].

---

[i] Congressional Thanksgiving Day Proclamation, Continental Congress, November 1, 1777

This first national Thanksgiving was celebrated Thursday, December 18<sup>th</sup>, 1777 and it was dedicated as a day of thanks for the victory of the Battle at Saratoga. This was only the beginning. Over the next decade congress issued several other national days for prayer, humiliation, and thanksgiving.

The next national declaration of Thanksgiving occurring on a Thursday in November was proclaimed November 26<sup>th</sup>, 1789 by George Washington:

> Whereas it is the duty of all Nations to acknowledge the providence of Almighty God, to obey his will, to be grateful for his benefits, and humbly to implore his protection and favor, and whereas both Houses of Congress have by their joint Committee requested me "to recommend to the People of the United States a day of public thanksgiving and prayer to be observed by acknowledging with grateful hearts the many signal favors of Almighty God especially by affording them an opportunity peaceably to establish a form of government for their safety and happiness.
>
> Now therefore I do recommend and assign Thursday the 26th day of November next to be devoted by the People of these States to the service of that great and glorious Being, who is the beneficent Author of all the good that was, that is, or that will be. That we may then all unite in rendering unto him our sincere and humble thanks, for his kind care and protection of the People of this Country previous to their becoming a Nation, for the signal and manifold mercies, and the favorable interpositions of his providence, which we experienced in the course and conclusion of the late war, for the great degree of tranquility, union, and plenty, which we have since enjoyed, for the peaceable and rational manner, in which we have been enabled to establish constitutions of government for our safety and happiness, and particularly the national One now lately instituted, for the civil and religious liberty with which we are blessed; and the means we have of acquiring and

diffusing useful knowledge; and in general for all the great and various favors which he hath been pleased to confer upon us[i].

These days of proclamation were not yet instituted every year, as the next was in 1795, then 1798 and 1799 under John Adams. Thomas Jefferson, the first non-believer to be counted among the presidents did not declare any days of Thanksgiving, though Madison, also not a Bible-believing Christian did see fit to renew congressional interest in a nationwide Thanksgiving and he proclaimed such a day in 1814, but the tradition of late November was not specifically linked to the proclamations of Thanksgiving.

After Madison, the national proclaiming of Thanksgiving days were not recorded, though most of the states declared special days independently. The next national proclamation was declared by Abraham Lincoln in the middle of the Civil War. Secretary of State William Seward wrote:

It has seemed to me fit and proper that they should be solemnly, reverently and gratefully acknowledged as with one heart and voice by the whole American people. I do therefore invite my fellow citizens in every part of the United States, and also those who are at sea and those who are sojourning in foreign lands, to set apart and observe the last Thursday of November next, as a day of Thanksgiving and Praise to our beneficent Father who dwelleth in the Heavens. And I recommend to them that while offering up the ascriptions justly due to Him for such singular deliverances and blessings, they do also, with humble penitence for our national perverseness and disobedience, commend to his tender care all those who have become widows, orphans, mourners or sufferers in the lamentable civil strife in which we are unavoidably engaged, and fervently implore the interposition of the Almighty Hand to heal the wounds of the nation and to restore it as soon as may be consistent with the Divine

---

[i]George Washington, October 3, 1789, Thanksgiving Proclamation

purposes to the full enjoyment of peace, harmony, tranquility and Union[i].

After this 1863 proclamation, Thanksgiving has been nationally celebrated every year in November.

The traditional date of Thanksgiving from Lincoln to Franklin D. Roosevelt was the last Thursday in November, but it was actually consumerism which called for a slight change in schedule. Roosevelt was still working to alleviate the Great Depression during his presidency spanning from 1933 to 1945. November 1933 had five Thursdays, and the last one was on the final day of the month leaving fewer weekends for the Christmas shopping season. The retail store leaders sent him letters asking for the official day to be set as the fourth Thursday of November which would help the economy by increasing the holiday shopping season and enabling stores to hire more employees. The culture at the time generally was unfavorable to Christmas decorations appearing before Thanksgiving (we can only dream of those days), and the retailers wanted an extra Saturday before Christmas. The letters went unheeded in 1933 and 1934 which both had five Thursdays, but in 1939 there was another five Thursdays in November during his presidency[ii]. Roosevelt this time sided with the retailers and declared the fourth Thursday of November for the 1939 Thanksgiving season which caused massive controversy. Football games would have to be rescheduled, family plans would have to change, and the opposing political party used this issue as a means to criticize the president (some things never change). This caused a split in the nation and the founding of a one-year holiday called Franksgiving Day. Thirty-two states and Washington DC celebrated Thanksgiving on the fourth Thursday while the remainder of the states observed the fifth Thursday. Two years later the matter was resolved by Congress and the Senate agreeing to affix the fourth

[i]Abraham Lincoln, October 3, 1863, Proclamation of Thanksgiving
[ii]How Did Thanksgiving End Up On The Fourth Thursday?, *NPR*, November 21, 2012

Thursday of November as the legal national holiday for Thanksgiving[i]. This allowed the post-depression merchants to set aside the famous day after Thanksgiving as the traditional start of the Christmas shopping sales season.

## THANKFUL FOR WHAT?

Christians in America have forgotten about Thanksgiving just as the rest of population has. I have not seen many Thanksgiving services or even references except small church dinners and those for the needy. Obviously the most serious of Christians give thanks to God daily, and still others give more thanks to God on Thanksgiving day. This is the model the Church should adopt as a whole, but we fear it does not happen because most church goers are not as interested in God as they may be in appearances, meeting nice people, or finding a weekly free rock concert. The root could be the lack of sound teaching in modern churches or a lack of faith in general. After all, if we lack faith, we do not realize there is a need to give thanks.

The Colonists breaking away from British control viewed many instances of God's provision and protection such that entire books have been written about the founding of the nation. Regarding Washington, in a single battle he had several bullet holes through his coat and lost two horses shot out from under him in battle yet he was unharmed. These and many more documented miracles in the founding of the United States led the founders to proclaim national days of Thanks. Even though our country has several problems, we still have enough freedom of religion in this country to worship as we see fit.

It may not always be as free to worship God as we presently enjoy, so we call on churches to talk more about our freedoms with deep praise during the Thanksgiving holiday. Yet, the American and other Western churches often take for granted the ownership of our Bibles. We live

---

[i]Congress Establishes Thanksgiving, *National Archives*, Accessed May 2019

in a time when we are allowed by law to own the holy books of our faith, and debate the matters of Christ in public. It was not always this way, as only 500 years ago the translation of the Bible into the common tongue of man was a capital offense. The pages of scripture are now legible to modern saints by the shedding of much blood. The greatest thanks we can give is to read our Bibles personally, and the greatest thanks the church can give is to encourage the congregation to meditate on the Word of God.

The other thanks we have in the Western society is general peace. We have more reminders of that in our modern world as we hear constant news of wars in the Middle East. Not all citizens of the world can safely walk down the street to the store or visit friends without the threat of crossfire, but let us not forget about the martyrs of our present world. According to the Voice of the Martyrs, Christians are still ravaged by martyrdom even today. Thousands of believers are put to death every year merely for the pronouncement of faith in Jesus. Yes, we in the West have a lot to be thankful for.

## But Are We Thankful?

Like all the rest of the American holidays, the real purpose behind Thanksgiving has been forgotten in the holiday hustle. Thanksgiving itself has even been squeezed out and trampled by the mad rush of Christmas sales. As we have seen, Thanksgiving itself was set on the fourth Thursday of November so as to not encroach on the Christmas sales season, so it is not a surprise that by 2012, big box retail stores disrupted Thanksgiving dinners all around the country, opening on Thursday afternoon. We are fortunate this caused the first glimmer of hope in consumer rebellion as opening big box stores so early became negative publicity. Subsequent years saw the retreat of Black Thursday sales back to Friday where the consumer beast belongs.

The loss of one day did not slow holiday spending and the amount we Americans spend has been steadily increasing. From 2014 to 2019 total annual retail sales increased from $375 billion to $451 billion. While these numbers are overwhelming, our interest is specifically in holiday sales. The National Retail Federation tracks holiday sales as a percentage of total annual sales and reports differences in trends. Holiday sales have been on the rise every year in recent decades except the 2008 market crash. Since 2010 when the markets began recovering, the annual holiday sales increased between 2-5% every year. The last numbers reported before the publication of this book indicate about $680 billion was spent in holiday sales between Thanksgiving and the end of the year.

Does this increase in spending mean people are not thankful? We do not necessarily think so, but we bring up these numbers to give you pause. When normalized to the American population, the average person was expected to spend about $1000 per person on holiday shopping. When we reflect on that number we should be asking if our spending was truly done because we felt compelled to spend due to the holiday demanding it, or if we spent out of genuine care. Certainly giving gifts is a form of love and we will examine who is in the best position to give gifts in our discussion on Christmas gifts, but if the holiday shopping has become a distraction from giving thanks to God or has caused your focus to dwell more on the expectations of the season, we should stop, repent, and return to God. Always be thankful whether it is giving gifts or just enjoying family times together.

## THE CALL FROM THE WORD

Our many blessings are also our downfall. God knows this is the progress of mankind's heart. Moses records the prediction about Israel's disobedience in *Deuteronomy 31:20*:

*For when I bring them into the land flowing with milk and honey, which I swore to their fathers, and they have eaten and are satisfied and become prosperous, then they will turn to other gods and serve them, and spurn Me and break My covenant.*

Even Joshua tells the people they are bent to serving other Gods:

*Then Joshua said to the people, "You will not be able to serve the LORD, for He is a holy God. He is a jealous God; He will not forgive your transgression or your sins. (Joshua 24:19)"*

The human reality is when things are going great we tend to forget about God. We see numerous cycles in the book of Judges where the people were doing great and so they strayed from God's commands. When they strayed, God sent their enemies to oppose and oppress His people causing them to call out to Him. This happened seven times in Judges where God would raise up a judge who would guide the people back into the direction God would have them go. It was the conflict, the pain, the turmoil that caused the Israelites to call on the name of God. Likewise, in our country it was during the turmoil of wars when Thanksgiving was incorporated, but now in times of peace our nation has forgotten it's meaning. When a nation remembers God and gives Him thanks and praise, the nation remains strong.

To contrast our fickle hearts which are prone to wander, Paul encourages us to:

*Be anxious for nothing, but in everything by prayer and supplication with thanksgiving let your requests be made known to God. And the peace of God, which surpasses all comprehension, will guard your hearts and your minds in Christ Jesus (Philippians 4:6-7).*

Our thankful hearts will help to guard our minds from the world. When we are constantly devoted to the love and power of Christ we are not drawn out into the sin of the world; but once we forget to give honor to the God of our provision it becomes easier to participate in the world around us.

Not only are we commanded to give thanks to God for our provision and protection against the sins of the world, but we are also given examples of thanksgiving for other believers. Paul opens his letter to the Ephesians proclaiming his thankfulness to them in his prayers. In this instance he is overjoyed with their salvation and praying God will give them knowledge of Christ:

> *For this reason I too, having heard of the faith in the Lord Jesus which exists among you and your love for all the saints, do not cease giving thanks for you, while making mention of you in my prayers; that the God of our Lord Jesus Christ, the Father of glory, may give to you a spirit of wisdom and of revelation in the knowledge of Him (Ephesians 1:15-17).*

And Paul also gives us a final exhortation in *1 Thessalonians 5:16-18*:

> *Rejoice always; pray without ceasing; in everything give thanks; for this is God's will for you in Christ Jesus.*

Our final model is to never stop giving thanks, whether that be the start of the Christmas shopping season or any other time in our life. When we stop remembering God we become less guarded against the schemes of the Devil. We should be thankful always, but on the national days of thanksgiving, we should declare all the more boldly the love we have for our savior and we should be thankful for our blessings whether we are in a free country or not. Never cease in giving thanks.

# Here Comes Satan Clause

## TOM'S CHRISTMAS PAST

I hate Christmas. I always have. Things, things, things. Sure as a child I wanted to get stuff like all kids, but the rest of the holiday always seemed too far away, something just out of touch. As an adult who is mostly utilitarian, it has been a bane of relatives who ask that haunting November question: "what do you want for Christmas?" Most years the answer is simply nothing, yet I still get things...every year...that mostly go to Goodwill, food banks, or my sometimes growing pot-belly. Since my conversion to Christ I have seen more farce in the Christmas season than holiness. I am not bothered that we celebrate our Savior's birthday on a day He likely was not born, but I am bothered that Christmas is more about the stuff than our new found life in Jesus Christ.

## TYLER'S CHRISTMAS PAST

Until I was 17, I never truly realized the meaning of Christmas. In the past, I've always seen Christmas and presents as a one way street: you give gifts to me. The culture teaches us this from a very early age and we naturally apply it to everything else, including holidays. I can look on Christmas's in the past and remember thinking "When will it be my turn open presents?" while my family was sitting in a big circle, these were the same years I also thought the church service that night was a massive waste of time and only interfered with my present opening time. I had Christmas tunnel vision and saw only one aspect, presents, as the only important thing, I never considered the bigger picture of family or Christ. We all get tied up by consumerism at some point in our lives, my weakest point was Christmas and like a lot of kids, I was too blinded by presents to see everything else wonderful happening that day.

## DEAD FROM CONSUMPTION

Christmas...the most ~~wonderful~~ consumer-focused time of the year. The central point of Christian worship should be Easter, and for many Christians it is, but on Christmas day, the most astute believers still focus on the birth of Jesus while the majority of America has been lulled into consumerism. Turning the love of Christ into the love of shopping, buying gifts for each other instead of offering ourselves up to Him, and hustling around to make sure everything is absolutely perfect for the Christmas gatherings. At these family get-togethers the focus usually becomes the gifts. Not our ultimate gift, but giving gifts to everyone. In fact, the season has become so synonymous with gift giving, the average American home does not typically give gifts out of love so much as from seasonal compulsion born from corporate America's marketing propaganda.

As we mentioned in the last chapter, the fourth Thursday in November was set as the national day for Thanksgiving specifically so the stores could start the big Christmas sales rush in plenty of time. The television programming, commercials, and movies in the post-

Thanksgiving time of the year all focus on what is for sale, what will fill our needs, and what will pull our heartstrings to buy that perfect gift (or 10) for every person in our life.

Like every other holiday, Christmas has suffered from consumption in the Western world. What started as a noble goal of shifting a pagan world from their own worship practices to honoring the birth of Jesus Christ in the newly established Christian Rome has again left the intended meaning behind in pursuit of cultural sentiment involving spending more money. Whether it be angels and crosses or Santa and reindeer anything that can sell us something becomes the new American focus.

Christmas is a complicated holiday. Some Christians will call us back to worship Christ more and other believers call us to abandon Christmas altogether as a mere devilish holiday. Others see Christmas as a time for family and gift exchanges. This complicated chapter will look at Western consumerism, American entertainment, pagan origins, and we will consider both sides of the discussion coming to a final culminating conclusion about how Christians should handle Christmas. Hold on tight because this chapter will move at rapid pace.

## GHOSTS OF CHRISTMAS PAST

### INITIAL CHRISTMAS CELEBRATIONS AND THE SATURNALIA CONNECTION

Saturnalia was a Roman festival celebrating the return of the sun after the shortening of the days in the winter months. The winter solstice is the shortest day of the year when the sun is the lowest in the sky. December 25th marked when the sun began to increase back in the horizon increasing daylight. The day was celebrated particularly by the lower class society and was marked by giving gifts to children, feasts, and general pagan conduct. This was not the only Pagan holiday in December. The Sigillaria,

Juvenalia, and Brumalia were also days in this season which the early Roman bishops combined all together for a single Christmas celebration in 360 AD in Rome. It is true, as some insinuate, that our modern Christmas celebrations do have a connection with the pagan holidays. The early church specifically chose to celebrate the birth of Christ on December 25th and find a way to justify that date later. They talked about the coming of the Son instead of the sun and correlated the giving of gifts to children with Christ receiving gifts from the magi. This also became the time period it was assumed three wise men came to Christ, and that at the time of His birth.

Pope Gregory was interested in removing pagan holidays from the Roman nation but he knew an outright ban would not accomplish this task. Converting the pagan festivals to Christian holidays was the best way to shift society from pagan practices to Christian observance without changing much more than sanitizing the old ways.

## THE BIRTH OF CHRIST

While Christmas time is the day modern Christians celebrate the birth, or better, incarnation of Christ, December is the least likely time for the actual birth of our savior. We know Jesus was born during the time of a Roman census (*Luke 2:1-6*). The records of the census were destroyed in 70AD when Jerusalem was burned so the records of the exact date were lost. We do know people had to travel to their city of origin during the census, and so such a census would have been issued during favorable travel days. December is a particularly cold season and so a census was not likely to be taken during this time of year.

On the night Jesus was born, angels announced the event to the shepherds who were keeping their flocks in the field:

*In the same region there were some shepherds staying out in the fields and keeping watch over their flock by night. And an angel of the Lord suddenly stood before them, and the glory of the Lord shone around them; and they were terribly frightened. But the angel said to them, "Do not be afraid; for behold, I bring you good news of great joy which will be for all the people; for today in the city of David there has been born for you a Savior, who is Christ the Lord. This will be a sign for you: you will find a baby wrapped in cloths and lying in a manger." (Luke 2:8-12)*

According to tradition, shepherds would keep flocks in the fields at night between the months of March and October. Of course exceptions could be made, but taken together with the census would lead us to believe Christ would have been born somewhere between March and November.

We personally would place the date around March for two key reasons. First, in ancient agricultural societies, the end of the year is a much busier time of the year because of multiple harvests, but in the early spring there is planting to be done before a lot of waiting. Secondly, it would make sense for the Lamb of God to be born in the spring time when ewe lambs were born.

As a man of such humble beginnings as to be cast from the inn and born in a stable, it is no surprise we are not privy to the date of Christ's birth. But that should not deter us from setting aside another day to honor Him. Such a thing was not commanded by the Scriptures, but neither is it forbidden. We see nothing wrong with setting aside a day in our culture to worship Christ, but we suggest herein Christmas is more for us than for Christ.

## CHRISTMAS TREE

The origins of the Christmas Tree are not scriptural, but it is one of the elements common in many pagan cultures. The tree was a part of the Saturnalia, but most cultures revered evergreen plants during the winter. As Paul declares in *Acts 17*, we are very religious people. Without verified revelation, we tend to manufacture our own gods. Most cultures have adapted sun worship and in the winter months the days get shorter leading many people to believe their sun god was becoming ill. The solstice marked the time when the days began growing longer. The people would decorate their houses with evergreen trees and wreaths to remind them of the time when all things would become green.

Early Christian traditions did not include the evergreen decorations as they sought to separate themselves from elements of the pagan holidays. Over the years, the pagan traditions mixed into the Christian holidays on that same day and the evergreens and wreaths were eventually added into may Christian homes.

The modern tradition of decorating evergreen trees began in Germany. Martin Luther was rumored to be the first to include lights on his tree. The story recounts he was walking through a grove one evening and saw stars glimmering through the evergreens. He enjoyed the appearance so much he decided that year to wire his own tree with candles to produce the same appearance at home. This legend notwithstanding, it does appear decorating trees with lights did first occur in Germany in the 1500s, though some trace it back to a wounded Swedish soldier in Germany which predates the Luther tradition. In this recounting, the Swedish tradition goes back many more centuries of decorating a tree with candies for the children. This Swedish officer is said to have thrown a Christmas party using an upright tree decorated with lights. The discrepancies, however, could be two separate traditions. In the Swedish culture, no mention is made of lights, but candies and the Luther account does not look at other decorations, merely lights on the tree. Of significance is that most traditions would have hung the tree upside down but both legends featured an upright tree. Regardless, it does appear our modern Christmas tree with decorations, lights, and candies on an upright tree does originate in Germany. In fact, it was the German immigrants who popularized

Christmas in America. We shall see more detail later about how the Puritans who first founded the colonies actually banned Christmas for a short period, but it was German influence which brought it back.

Ultimately, while the initial décor including evergreens was associated with the Saturnalia among other celebrations and cultures, it was accepted in many Christian circles and those believers even added to the traditions by adding lights to the trees to signify the coming of Christ.

## GIFT GIVING

Gift giving was first observed in the festivals surrounding the Saturnalia. Some traditions say gifts were given on December 19th on the Sigillaria but other traditions indicate gifts were given over the course of several days at the conclusion of meals. Children received toys but the adults would receive pottery, figurines, and gag gifts to demonstrate humor. It would be difficult to tell if the gags related to gift giving was a genuine interest in joviality or if it was more related to the excess of public drunkenness.

As the celebrations wore on leading to the Christianization of Rome, the early church fathers supplanted the gift-giving aspect of the Saturnalia with parallels in the Christian faith: namely the giving of gifts by the wise men. Since we have already moved the birth of Christ to December, it also paved the way for two more wide-spread fallacies, first being there were three wise men, based on the three gifts. The only Gospel making reference to the wise men is the book of Matthew, which merely points to a plurality of magi (*Matthew 2:1*). This was likely a caravan with numerous people, but the Scriptures are silent. We only know three distinct gifts were presented to Joseph and Mary as the parents of Jesus.

The second fallacy is the magi visited Jesus when he was born. This is most likely confused in that Luke provides the fine details about the birth of Christ, but is silent on the wise men. Matthew details the magi in more detail but is silent on His birth. The best examination we can say about the appearance of the magi is they appeared in Jerusalem when Jesus was about 2 years old. We can say this is reasonable because Matthew reports the time of the appearance of the star would have appeared about two years prior to the arrival of the Magi, and that star was linked to His birth (*Matthew 2:16*).

The importance of this in the ancient traditions is while the pagan festival appeared for a week beginning on our modern December 17th, the early church fathers combined the magi, gifts, and birth of Christ and used that as a means to justify giving gifts during the newly created Christmas holiday. The irony of this celebration is that Jesus was not likely born on December 25th, the wise men did not see Him on the day He was born, but the presentation of Gold, Frankincense, and Myrrh serve to justify the old pagan ways under the guise of Christian teaching.

## SANTA

Santa as we see him today is a modern cultural icon stemming from Saint Nicholas, also known as Nikolaos of Myra and Nicholas of Bari. He was a devout Christian, of at least the second generation in his family and he lived during the Roman prosecutions being released from Prison when Constantine pardoned all Christians and set up Rome as a Christian nation.

Saint Nicholas was born in 270 or 280 to wealthy Christian parents who died while He was still young, Nicholas inherited their great wealth, and he chose even from a very early age to give from his wealth to people in need. Even as a teenager he secretly paid the dowry prices for a poor man's three daughters so they would not grow up in prostitution. He eventually felt called into the ministry and went to the monastery near Myra to study until the high priest there received a vision that Nicholas was to be ordained as a bishop. He served as the Bishop in Myra after his studies at the monastery. Nicholas held the Scriptures faithfully even in his early years battling the false god, Artemis, in his local jurisdiction. In 303 he was arrested by decree from Diocletian and tortured in Prison. Nicholas was mostly likely released from prison around 313 when Constantine decriminalized Christianity.

Nicholas was known by his congregation for his holiness and zeal for the true Christ found in the Scriptures and also for his preaching against false teachers which kept the Arian heresy from his congregation. Nicholas also appeared at the Council of Nicaea where tradition said he attacked Arius for his unfaithfulness to the Scriptures.

Nicholas used his wealth as a young man to save the three daughters mentioned above. There are some other legends appearing later in history about saving children from an evil merchant, but other verified stories of gift giving was the spark to create the persona of Nicholas, the gift giver. The first gift was enough to teach the lessons on generous giving from a wealthy bishop and many cultures have developed traditions about a gift giver to bless the children whom are well behaved, almost all seem to be based on the Bishop of Myra. The English have Father Christmas, the Dutch have adopted Sinterklaas.

Sinterklass was one of the primary influences for Santa Claus, the difference is Sinter was around 300 years prior, but also rooted in Saint Nicholas. They have plenty of crossed paths through the tales, accomplishments, and appearances their revamped versions hold, they also both love to help children. A common story shared between the two follows three beautiful daughters who want to marry higher class boys they like, unfortunately, their lower status doesn't allow them to even meet them. Sinterklaas sends Grumpus, his servant, to give the ladies 100 Ducats each to pay the dowry to marry them. Also similar to Saint Nicholas is their status of Bishop over Myra in the 4$^{th}$ century, this sets them up as the good ruler everyone should strive to be. We see these are two culturally distinct interpretations of the same faithful Christian man.

## CHRISTMAS DÉCOR

Besides the Christmas displays found in supermarkets, the signs of the season begin to appear in the form of decorations in people's yards and doors. Christmas wreaths and mistletoe are not new additions to the holidays any more than Jesus or the Christmas tree. The hanging of these and other plants have ancient traditions as old or older than the Saturnalia itself.

When the days began to shrink, the druids of old religions would assume the sun was sick causing the land to fail. This led to the practice of bringing specific plants into the house during the Winter Solstice on December 21$^{st}$, the shortest day of the year. The druidic cultures believed in spirits attached to every plant and by bringing holly, mistletoe, ivy, and evergreens into ones home they believed they were giving the spirits of those plants safe lodging for the time when the land was weak.

The holly and mistletoe specifically were supposed to bring good luck and by hanging it high on the doorframe good luck would be able to enter but the bad luck will be driven off. The wreaths, often made of pine and other evergreens intertwined with ivy, were a symbol of life that continued to press on despite the ill state of the rest of the land. Such décor was a sign that fertile life was to press on throughout the season.

The next tradition is that of the Yule Log. This is more of a British and European tradition which has not caught on in the United States in most regions, although it is possible Christmas lights may have a root in this tradition. The practice appears to begin as a Nordic tradition where the family would select a tree and cut it down, bringing it into the house to burn. The log was lit from a fire made with the remains of the prior year's log symbolizing the troubles of the past year to be burned and the new year to begin. The tree was to be burned over the course of the twelve days of Christmas starting with the previous year's remains and then over the course of the next twelve days it was to be continuously burned. Anything that remained after the twelve days of Christmas was saved to start the fire the following year. The ashes produced by burning the log were also saved and mixed with the soil at the start of the year to provide fertilizer to the crops giving the ancient people a belief this practice helped produce good luck in the growing of the crops.

## CHRISTMAS OVER THE AGES

Like the rest of the holidays we have discussed, Christmas is unrecognizable from the pagan traditions that were later converted to Christianity. As the namesake of Jesus' birth, Christmas has the reputation of the most important holiday to the Christian, possibly sharing that honor with Easter. But our current view of Christmas has morphed into something unrecognizable.

We have already seen the early worship at Saturnalia and we have mentioned how Pope Gregory Christianized several of the Pagan holidays in an effort to weed out the old worship and replace it with the new. Pope Gregory was the leader of the church during those days when people moved to worship God out of compulsion rather than the love of their savior. This marked the dark days of inquisitions, crusades, and people put to death for the simple crime of not believing in the state religion.

As Catholicism spread in the dark days of the church, the priests began to place more focus on days of saints, relics, and population control. The festivals were considered divinely appointed and penalties were initiated against those who chose not to celebrate. Despite the forced celebration of this and other religious actions, Augustine,

Jerome, and others insisted all celebration was supposed to be a matter of the heart and not compulsion, but the leaders of the church won out and persecuted those who would not partake in festivities. Sadly partaking devolved into the types of celebrations common among the Greeks including drunkenness and debauchery in many areas, thus the pagan rituals of Rome were Christianized under the prevailing church of the day.

By the time of the reformers, the protestant congregations began separating themselves from everything the church in Rome required of society. The pockets of reformation leadership sought to separate the universal church from the Roman church including the calendar, saint's days, and the celebrations in favor of a simpler Christian calendar with remembrance of the Lord rising on Sunday morning. This would mean a reduction in forced celebrations which included the Christmas festivities. The result in reformation-laden populations was the pendulum swung too far the other direction leading to persecution of people who chose to celebrate Christmas.

It was this spirit of separation that made it illegal to celebrate Christmas in America under the rule of the separatists. From 1659 to 1681, decorating, worshiping, or doing anything special on Christmas day was outlawed in Boston and the surrounding New England colonies. To be caught celebrating the holiday season in any way resulted in a 5 shilling fine. This, however, was isolated as the Jamestown settlement allowed and openly celebrated the seasonal festivities. Regardless, Christmas was not a national holiday until a century later when congress declared Christmas a federal holiday on June 26th, 1870. Since this time the modern holiday was transformed from what amounted to a pagan holiday of debauchery into the family-friendly holiday we celebrate today.

## CHRISTMAS AT GROUND ZERO

It's so strange how Christmas tradition can prevail in the most dire of times, especially in the middle of an intense stalemate on the Western front, one of the most arduous battles of all time. The era is WWI, and clashing weapons were ceased a month in December 1914 when the German and British troops planned an unofficial Christmas celebration dubbed 'The Christmas Truce'[i]. This happened against the wishes of their superiors, who were reluctant to participate until the sweet cease-fire caused them to join in the German carols. The troops starting singing about 8:30am from the trenches to kick off the event. The eyewitness accounts recall lights illuminating German trenches and a cease of all aggression by the British was met with some whiskey and a cigar by the Germans. Who could resist that? These acts of kindness were carried along by the British, who sang their own carols. It was a wondrous day, reportedly there was a feast of rations with soldiers telling their stories of how they became involved in the war. They shared stories of their families from the comfort of the German trenches. Similar Christmas parties happened around the battlefront between December 11th to the 26th, dates corresponding to the Jewish holiday Hanukkah. If such peace and celebration can be found in a battlefield of all places, perhaps we can all find peace through Christmas.

## GHOSTS OF CHRISTMAS PRESENT

### SHOPPING SEASON

Joel Waldfogel is called a scrooge by many, particularly since he wrote the book called *Scroogenomics: Why You Shouldn't Buy Presents for the Holidays*. He argues in the book that on the principle of monetary loss alone, the cost to consumers dwarfs the waste of the most callous government spending. We talked about the very setting of the

---

[i]The Story of the WWI Christmas Truce, *The Smithsonian*, December 23, 2011

Thanksgiving day was directly related to the Christmas shopping season as it was once anathema to decorate for Christmas or begin Christmas sales until after the Thanksgiving holiday. Thus the entire Christmas shopping season is more about buying things than it is the warm fuzzies of giving. We consumers can become taken in by the deals, the sales, or even the random bins of cheap-quality useless Christmas junk like the mini billiard table, the beer-bottle golf club cover, and cheap trinkets of the passing year's most prominent movie characters.

Waldfogel placed consumer holiday spending at between $53-$95 billion in 2007, the last year of stats before he published his book. Of course that was right before a major economic crisis, but he also indicates signs then (as occur now) that the government still encourages people to go out and spend. The most famous example of this was after the September 11 attacks, the stock market totally tanked (Tom was a small time investor at the time and he lost over half of his investments), and President Bush appeared on television encouraging Americans to keep spending and to go on as if nothing had happened. And go on we do. Dave Ramsey takes regular calls from people who are deeply in debt and helps them get out of the hole they have dug for themselves. He observes every year whether money is tight or savings have been made, people still buy too many gifts for their kids, and they usually charge those gifts to a credit card.

The problem here, according to Waldfogel, is that most of the Christmas spending for gifts is devalued in that the majority of our giving is not what a person would have bought themselves if they had the opportunity. This means if Grandma buys a gift at a cost of $50 for little Johnny, the gift may not have the $50 valuation if it is not something Johnny specifically wanted. To break this down in a more real way, the closer the relation to the recipient, the higher the gift valuation becomes. A parent, spouse, or child generally gets a higher monetary valuation for gifts than does a great aunt or Grandma, unless, of course, Grandma buys Johnny exactly what Johnny says to buy. This, according to Waldfogel, means that it is best to save our gift giving exclusively to those we share the greatest relationships and not worry about finding a gift for your great uncle.

## THE WHITE ELEPHANT GIFT EXCHANGE IN THE ROOM

The White Elephant Gift Exchange is probably our least favorite part of the modern Christmas season. Our reasons are not because of the Saturnalia connection, but rather because it is likely the most wasteful part of spending in the Christmas season...even if it is only five dollars!

To explain, we first want to denounce the view that everything must be of real economic value. Our prior section looked at monetary waste in the Christmas season, and from the perspective of an economist, the cost of holiday spending does not equate to the gain of satisfaction and is thus wasteful. The economic loss is not our reason, either. Certainly money can be spent on a good time. Movie going is not a waste if one enjoys the movie, and perhaps some see the white elephant exchange in the same light: buy some small, silly item and then see whose contribution results in the most laughs. That could certainly be a reason to participate.

However, our perspective is a mass combination of the sheer number of such parties combined with the necessity to buy a gift that will have zero impact on the recipient, and then it just adds to the things we buy and do not need or worse, buy and cannot afford. Thus, the white elephant exchange, while being a cheap gift, is one without redeeming value, increasing both financial and real waste, all for a few laughs. We would rather keep that money, not enrich the corporate stores a bit more, and spend some real time with family and friends in different ways over the holiday season.

### CHRISTMAS DÉCOR

Our modern Christmas decorations bear a little resemblance to the old traditions, but they have taken on a life of their own. In one of the most remarkable marketing campaigns of all time, the Coca-cola company combined the new fizzy drink with the traditions of Saint Nick, Father Christmas, and others to create the character we now know as Santa. Indeed, the jolly old man did gain his weight through the marketing campaign as the soda company envisioned a jolly old man as the giver of gifts. Since that time the fantasies of the north pole, elves, and reindeer have taken hold. The nativity of Jesus was sectioned off to Churches while Santa Clause has usurped the position of the great gift giver.

We still decorate the Christmas Tree which holds its roots in the Saturnalia, middle age church, and some of the early reformers. To say we decorate the tree to worship the god Saturn would certainly be fallacy because like everything else in the Christmas season it has been born out of our culture more than from our faith.

Even though Santa, Frosty, and the reindeer have taken such a prominent position in the Christmas decorations, it is still nice to see the angels and nativities still mostly accepted, and thus is a part of the reason why many people choose to attend a Christmas service even when they do not give God a second chance most of the year.

The final verdict of the Christmas décor is that it is neither Christian nor Pagan, it is part of who we are as a society. Like the old days when the Children's eyes would light up as the annual festival approached, we can celebrate the joy on the faces and in the hearts of our children. We should not ban the Christmas tree because of a connection to the Saturnalia but we should not attempt to justify every symbol as a part of Christian history. While some families teach there is not a Santa, others let the little children believe it. Let the Christmas decorations be what they are and enjoy the season with sobriety.

## ENTERTAINMENT

Tyler is a big fan of cheesy and somewhat bad films. Whether it be *Turbo Man* or *Kung Fury*, bad movies are so fun! Some of the best of the worst are the beloved 'Christian' movies, usually trying very hard, yet bad acting and low budget get in the way of the Godly message. As followers of Christ who are reasonably knowledgeable in God's Word, the very idea of these cinematic adventures getting any recognition from Christians is both hilarious and disheartening, and nothing peaks our interest more in this area than *Kirk Cameron's Saving Christmas*, which is a hoot! People on the secular side seem to collectively think the movie is absolutely ridiculous. On one hand, we share those thoughts, but we are also saddened by the film's claims. This production tries to blur the lines between secular and Christian Christmas ideals, which we should be separating more in this day of rampant consumerism. This film suggests God decorated the Garden of Eden with lights for Christmas, that Saint Nicholas was a brawler who beat up the establishment to give to the kids on Christmas, and that we should see the cross every time we see a Christmas Tree. Cameron was trying too hard combine Christian and secular values in one movie. He is a fellow Christian brother, and because of that we can't fault him for attempting to expand the kingdom, but in this world, we need to take extra steps to differentiate ourselves from the pagan society around us.

*Ecclesiastes 3:4* promptly states there to a time to weep and a time to laugh, a time to mourn and a time to dance. We can laugh at the movie for a short time, but we eventually have to mourn because of the state of modern Christianity. We pray Cameron can realize God can influence his own path through film without the meaning of Christmas changing. The modern church movement of 'changing for the culture' and 'incorporating the culture so this pill is easier to swallow' is an extremely flawed system, an example of this is the producer's attempt to combine two colliding worlds into one film.

The Christmas of Godly folk and the Christmas of secular folk should be segregated; they're two different beasts with different motives, characters, and ideology. The film fails, though with good intention, to make Christmas better for some demographics. Sadly, Kirk Cameron has become a mark of tokenism in Hollywood; He is just one example of a larger trend in film production. We don't doubt him or anyone making similar properties is not a Christian or has good intentions, but they need to realize what they are representing; Christ on earth. Let this be a cautionary tale and warning about the dangers of some modern Christian movies, particularly those around the season.

### TYLER REFLECTS ON CHURCH SERVICES

My (Tyler) opinion of Christmas has changed like most people growing up. I used to see the Church service as interfering with my time opening presents, and what kids doesn't? But as I grew up and place my own true faith in God, I started seeing our Christmas service as something special. I always attended the Christmas Eve service at my grandmom's church and have learned to really appreciate it.

Expanding on the church service that night for the entire chapter would be boring, but I think It's important to understand where I'm coming from when writing this as a convert to true Christianity. We enter the church, and the first thing we do is pick up a candle per person, we go in and it's like your standard Sunday service until the last 30 minutes when we turn off the lights and use the candles we grabbed at the beginning to light up the sanctuary while singing *Silent Night.* I don't know if that's the common agenda for all of the Christmas services around America, but it is by far the best service out of the whole year. Between the atmosphere of reverence and the above average sermon from the preacher, this encapsulates everything I love about a Godly church, only if it was like this in every service throughout the year! I notice more often the church (and Christianity as a whole) is merging with cultural ideas and beliefs more so each passing year, and even though I occasionally make fun of and even cynically enjoy the state of the modern church, no matter what way we cut it, this 'get hip with the evil world' mentality is destroying every single inch of the western church and what it formerly believed. Consider the words of the Apostle Paul:

*Preach the word; be ready in season and out of season; reprove, rebuke, exhort, with great patience and instruction. For the time will come when they will not endure sound doctrine; but wanting to have their ears tickled, they will accumulate for themselves teachers in accordance to their own desires, and will turn away their ears from the truth and will turn aside to myths (2 Timothy 4:2-4).*

When the church starts blatantly disobeying God's word to score culture points we have arrived at Paul's conclusion. This is important to consider in the context of the Christmas service because it and Easter seem in many congregations to be the final stronghold to pure infestation of the church with cultural norms. We, as believers, are not holding firm to sound doctrines and rather, flock to sermons that make us feel good. Let us remember Christ is the center of Christianity and following Him is about denying ourselves. Learn from these few remaining services that the Gospel is more important than Christmas gifts!

## GHOSTS OF CHRISTMAS FUTURE

Christmas doesn't need to be as controversial as we make it out to be. It is certainly true there are elements of the holiday associated with old paganism but it is also true that most of Christendom has endorsed and celebrates Christmas for many good reasons. We also know modern Western Christmas has a whole lot more to do with consumerism than it does tradition, religion, or Christ. Does that mean we can celebrate the day or should we borrow the religious zeal of the separatists and make Christmas illegal outright? The final sections of this chapter will answer these questions.

## TO PARTAKE OR NOT?

Some religious communities including the Jehovah's Witnesses do not celebrate Christmas at all. Others who identify as Christian also reject the seasonal festivities merely on the basis of the Saturnalia connections. We know the early reformers who had a hand in settling the colonies in Massachusetts rejected the Christmas traditions merely because of the connection to Roman Catholicism. These reasons are not enough to answer our questions. We should never celebrate a day merely because someone says to (unless that person is God), and likewise we should not turn away from such a day on similar pretense. Rather, we should examine the Scriptures and examine the event to determine what is the heart behind it. As Paul writes to the Thessalonians:

> *Examine everything carefully, hold fast to that which is good, abstain from every evil thing (1 Thessalonians 5:21-22).*

So let us examine the day and the Scriptures to determine if we can celebrate Christmas.

The first consideration is whether the practice of Christmas is sinful. The best place to start is to look at the deeds of the flesh found in *Galatians 5:19-21*:

> *Now the deeds of the flesh are evident, which are: immorality, impurity, sensuality, idolatry, sorcery, enmities, strife, jealousy, outbursts of anger, disputes, dissensions, factions, envying, drunkenness, carousing, and things like these, of which I forewarn you, just as I have forewarned you, that those who practice such things will not inherit the kingdom of God.*

This general list of sinful behaviors will allow us to ask if Christmas is all about anything on this list. While it is true that Christmas can cause some of these feelings, it would be a stretch to say Christmas is all about these sins. We do find elements of jealousy, envying, and in some families, fights. But Christmas in our culture is more about gifts, family, and consumerism. While we are not big fans of consumerism, it is not a sin described in the Bible either by verse nor concept. Taken together, we believe it is permissible on a Biblical level to celebrate Christmas so long as your own conscience has not convinced you otherwise.

Another consideration is whether or not we are forbidden from celebrating secular festivities at all. The answer to this question is a little more difficult because we have little in the Bible about this occurrence. We know the early church fathers had a problem with the gladiatorial games, but that was more likely due to the violence surrounding the event. We hear the phrase, "in the world but not of the world" in our modern churches, but the phrase is not uttered in Scripture. We know we are dual citizens and we need to acknowledge the commands of both lands, not allowing the freedoms of one culture to lead us into rebellion in the other.

## A CALL TO RIGHTEOUS CHRISTMAS

Our final conclusion about Christmas is that we should be focusing more on God and the ultimate gift of Jesus Christ and less on the cultural expectations placed on us from family, society, and businesses. If we are so inclined to purchase gifts for those we love, we should exercise that right to the glory of God. If we are instead to focus on who Jesus is and leave out gift giving all together, we ought to allow someone the freedom to do just that without regard for expectations.

We feel this is the similar case with Christmas parties, white elephant exchanges, and other cultural aspects of the season. Our primary focus for this and all holidays should be in the ultimate gift giver, Jesus Christ, and the salvation He has given us. While we celebrate our common salvation, we should neither turn to the one fallacy saying Christmas is all about Jesus born in a stable on Christmas morning, nor should we discount the festivities as a mere pagan construct. Christmas as we know it is a cultural thing and as Christians, we are free to engage in the practice or to not, each choice being to the glory of God.

# Old Testament Holidays

God gave the Israelites specific feasts they had to celebrate or else they would be cut off from the community. These feasts required specific days of rest and sacrifices. The most important of these was the Feast of the Unleavened Bread, during which the Passover was remembered. The other two major feasts were the start of the growing season (Feast of Harvest, Feast of Weeks) and the harvest time (Feast of the Ingathering).

The three prescribed feasts were to be celebrated by all people in the nation, and the celebration was to occur at a specific place. During the writing of the law, Moses recorded the celebration was to be held at *the place where the LORD your God chooses to establish His name (Deuteronomy 16:6). 2 Chronicles 6:5-6* names that location as Jerusalem. *Deuteronomy 16:16-17* commands all males to make a pilgrimage to Jerusalem three times a year. By extension from other scriptures, the family also traveled with the men who presented offerings for themselves and their families. So among the feasts prescribed throughout the year, three of them required a pilgrimage and a significant sacrifice.

### PASSOVER (FIRST SABBATH OF THE FEAST OF UNLEAVENED BREAD)

God chose to demonstrate His power to His chosen people, Israel, the Egyptians, and the surrounding nations. Moses was commanded by God to go back to his people and confront Pharaoh to let the Israelites go from the bondage in the land of Goshen. When Pharaoh refused to let the people go, God demonstrated His ultimate authority in the form of ten plagues, all direct assaults on the false gods of Egypt. The Passover was the final plague; a discriminate killing of the first born of Egypt. The Passover and Feast of Unleavened Bread were an annual commemoration that the Israelites were once enslaved in a foreign land, but were released by the mighty hand of God.

The Passover was prescribed in detail in *Exodus 12:3-11*:

*Speak to all the congregation of Israel, saying, 'On the tenth of this month they are each one to take a lamb for themselves, according to their fathers' households, a lamb for each household. Now if the household is too small for a lamb, then he and his neighbor nearest to his house are to take one according to the number of persons in them; according to what each man should eat, you are to divide the lamb. Your lamb shall be an unblemished male a year old; you may take it from the sheep or from the goats. You shall keep it until the fourteenth day of the same month, then the whole assembly of the congregation of Israel is to kill it at twilight. Moreover, they shall take some of the blood and put it on the two doorposts and on the lintel of the houses in which they eat it. They shall eat the flesh that same night, roasted with fire, and they shall eat it with unleavened bread and bitter herbs. Do not eat any of it raw or boiled at all with water, but rather roasted with fire, both its head and its legs along with its entrails. And you shall not leave any of it over until morning, but whatever is left of it until morning, you shall burn with fire. Now you shall eat it in this manner: with your loins girded, your sandals on your feet, and your staff in your hand; and you shall eat it in haste—it is the LORD'S Passover.*

In God's prescription for the Passover, each family was to select an unblemished lamb on the 10th day of the month. If the families were too small to consume a full lamb, they were to share it with their neighbors. The whole community would slaughter their lamb at twilight on the 14th day of the month, the day before the Sabbath. The blood spilled while slaughtering the lamb was to be painted on the doorposts and lintel of the house with hyssop (*Exodus 12:22*). The lamb was to be roasted whole, including the organs, and it was to be roasted with bitter herbs to symbolize the bitter slavery in Egypt. Jewish tradition holds the herbs to be horseradish, romaine lettuce, or endives, but Scripture does not tell us for sure. The people were to consume all of the lamb by morning, and whatever they could not eat was to be completely burned. Also, the people were commanded to eat the lamb with their robe and staff as if ready for a journey.

During the first Passover, the destroying angel God sent to kill the firstborn of Egypt would pass over every house touched by the blood of the Passover sacrifice. This was the first sign to the nation of Israel that a prescribed sacrifice could cause differentiation between people. Every year they were to repeat the sacrifice as a remembrance of their past enslavement and subsequent delivery from Goshen in Egypt.

## FEAST OF UNLEAVENED BREAD

Leaven is frequently stated as being a metaphor for sin, and some sites callously state that yeast means sin in the Old Testament, but supporting verses are mysteriously absent. Yeast, however, is used in a small amount and grows throughout the bread, so it is more often used to illustrate rapid growth, though Paul does use it as a metaphor for how easy sin can take us over, he also uses leaven in a similarly positive context (*1 Corinthians 5:6-8*). Likewise, when Jesus speaks of the Leaven of the Pharisees in *Matthew 16:6-12*, he was not speaking of sin, but how such a small trace of false teaching can pollute the whole person. Because we are sinners it is easy to compare yeast to sin owing to our festering nature, regardless, that is not why the Israelites were commanded to remove yeast from their houses. It had more to do with the haste by which they needed to prepare and consume the meal. If one were to make a simple flatbread without yeast it can be made in a few minutes, but even with our modern technology it takes a few hours to make a loaf with yeast. Thus, the unleavened bread was to commemorate the haste the Israelites had to leave Egypt.

Moses delivered the commands regarding the week of unleavened bread in *Exodus 12:14-20*:

> 'Now this day will be a memorial to you, and you shall celebrate it as a feast to the LORD; throughout your generations you are to celebrate it as a permanent ordinance. Seven days you shall eat unleavened bread, but on the first day you shall remove leaven from your houses; for whoever eats anything leavened from the first day until the seventh day, that person shall be cut off from Israel. On the first day you shall have a holy assembly, and another holy assembly on the seventh day; no work at all shall be done on them, except what must be eaten by every person, that alone may be prepared by you. You shall also observe the Feast of Unleavened Bread, for on this very day I brought your hosts out of the land of Egypt; therefore you shall observe this day throughout your generations as a permanent ordinance. In the first month, on the fourteenth day of the month at evening, you shall eat unleavened bread, until the twenty-first day of the month at evening. Seven days there shall be no leaven found in your houses; for whoever eats what is leavened, that person shall be cut off from the congregation of Israel, whether he is an alien or a native of the land. You shall not eat anything leavened; in all your dwellings you shall eat unleavened bread.'"

On the Sabbath day everyone in Israel had to remove the yeast from their tent. Tradition says they buried it outside the boundaries of their residence. Bread was to be eaten throughout the week without any yeast. The first and the last day was a Sabbath rest and anyone who ate leavened bread was to be cut off from the community, and this included slaves and foreigners. In addition to removing the yeast from the houses, the people were required to offer a sacrifice. The men would offer the sacrifice on behalf of themselves and their families; it included two bulls, a ram, seven male lambs, a grain offering, and a goat as a sin offering. The week was one of celebration, but work could be done in between the Sabbaths, the people only had the command to abstain from leavened bread.

After midnight on the night of the Passover, Pharaoh summoned Moses and Aaron and told them to flee the land immediately. The people of Israel arose late in the night before their bread had rose and fled Egypt (*Exodus 12:34*). Thus the command to remove yeast from their houses during the feast after the Passover was a remembrance of the haste by which the people fled Goshen.

## FEAST OF FIRST FRUITS, FEAST OF WEEKS

Many ancient religions hold a celebration marking specific times during their year. The two most important annual feasts in most agricultural societies have always been the start and the end of the harvest. For the Israelites, there are two days marked as the start of the gathering of the grains and one of them is bound up with the Passover and the Feast of Unleavened Bread. The Passover was on a Friday, the next day, the Sabbath, was the Feast of Unleavened Bread, and the following Sunday was the Feast of First Fruits. The Feast of Weeks came several weeks later. Both of these feasts were celebrated in Jerusalem, the first, Feast of the First Fruits, marked the beginning of the barley harvest, and the second, the Feast of Weeks, marked the beginning of the wheat harvest.

*Leviticus 23:9-13* describes the Feast of First Fruits:

> Then the LORD spoke to Moses, saying, "Speak to the sons of Israel and
> say to them, 'When you enter the land which I am going to give to you
> and reap its harvest, then you shall bring in the sheaf of the first fruits
> of your harvest to the priest. He shall wave the sheaf before the LORD
> for you to be accepted; on the day after the sabbath the priest shall
> wave it. Now on the day when you wave the sheaf, you shall offer a
> male lamb one year old without defect for a burnt offering to the LORD.
> Its grain offering shall then be two-tenths of an ephah (2.18 quarts) of
> fine flour mixed with oil, an offering by fire to the LORD for a soothing
> aroma, with its drink offering, a fourth of a hin (pint) of wine.

The three days of celebration in Israel started with
reaping the first grains of the barley harvest, but they were
not to cook any bread from the grains until after the offering
(*Leviticus 23:14*). The Sunday after the Feast of Unleavened
Bread, the man of the household would offer the sheaf of
barley to the priest. The accompanying sacrifice included a
lamb from the flock, flour, oil, and wine. It is of note that
these commands were given to Israel shortly after the
departure from Egypt, but they would not finally offer this
feast for another forty years after the desert wanderings. It
was to be instituted only once they had received their
inheritance (*Leviticus 23:9*).

The growing season was divided between the quickly
sprouting barley and the slower growing wheat. The Feast of
First Fruits celebrated the first crop of the barley feast, but a
set period of time later the people would make another
pilgrimage back to Jerusalem to offer the first of the wheat
harvest. The second feast, the Feast of Weeks, was a larger
sacrifice and is described in *Leviticus 23:15-19*:

> 'You shall also count for yourselves from the day after the sabbath, from
> the day when you brought in the sheaf of the wave offering; there shall
> be seven complete sabbaths. You shall count fifty days to the day after
> the seventh sabbath; then you shall present a new grain offering to the
> LORD. You shall bring in from your dwelling places two loaves of bread

*for a wave offering, made of two-tenths of an ephah; they shall be of a
fine flour, baked with leaven as first fruits to the LORD. Along with the
bread you shall present seven one year old male lambs without defect,
and a bull of the herd and two rams; they are to be a burnt offering to
the LORD, with their grain offering and their drink offerings, an offering
by fire of a soothing aroma to the LORD. You shall also offer one male
goat for a sin offering and two male lambs one year old for a sacrifice of
peace offerings. The priest shall then wave them with the bread of the
first fruits for a wave offering with two lambs before the LORD; they are
to be holy to the LORD for the priest. On this same day you shall make a
proclamation as well; you are to have a holy convocation. You shall do
no laborious work. It is to be a perpetual statute in all your dwelling
places throughout your generations.*

This day was rigidly set as seven Sabbaths and 50 days
after the Feast of the Harvest. While the first feast, just at the
start of the growing season, was a small required sacrifice
including the first of the barley, some flour, wine, and a
lamb as a burnt offering, the second feast was much larger.
The people were to present two loaves of bread (forbidden
in the first feast as part of the Feast of Unleavened Bread),
seven lambs, two rams, and a bull. This was also a time for
collecting the first tithe, most likely the tithe on the barley
which the harvest was now over. The tithe was used as a
great feast celebrated by all of the people.

Taken together, the Feast of Harvest and the Feast of
Weeks commemorated the beginning of the harvest and
celebrated the provisions that God would grant them for
their year of obedience. Both feasts required a gathering in
Jerusalem which, as we shall show later, is significant in the
life of the Christian, and they both required males to attend.

## FEAST OF BOOTHS

Like other agricultural societies, the Israelites also
celebrated the end of the harvest, but unlike other nations,

they had specific commands about their worship. The end of the growing season meant they now received an abundance of grains and an increase in cattle. Thus the tithes were instituted to share the burden of the people in society whom were not as successful. God promised the nation as a whole would remain fertile if the people only obeyed His commands (*Deuteronomy 28:1-14*). This was the tithe of the cattle and the final tithe of the crops. God outlined the feast in *Leviticus 23:33-43*:

> Again the LORD spoke to Moses, saying, "Speak to the sons of Israel, saying, 'On the fifteenth of this seventh month is the Feast of Booths for seven days to the LORD. On the first day is a holy convocation; you shall do no laborious work of any kind. For seven days you shall present an offering by fire to the LORD. On the eighth day you shall have a holy convocation and present an offering by fire to the LORD; it is an assembly. You shall do no laborious work.

> 'These are the appointed times of the LORD which you shall proclaim as holy convocations, to present offerings by fire to the LORD—burnt offerings and grain offerings, sacrifices and drink offerings, each day's matter on its own day— besides those of the sabbaths of the LORD, and besides your gifts and besides all your votive and freewill offerings, which you give to the LORD.

> 'On exactly the fifteenth day of the seventh month, when you have gathered in the crops of the land, you shall celebrate the feast of the LORD for seven days, with a rest on the first day and a rest on the eighth day. Now on the first day you shall take for yourselves the foliage of beautiful trees, palm branches and boughs of leafy trees and willows of the brook, and you shall rejoice before the LORD your God for seven days. You shall thus celebrate it as a feast to the LORD for seven days in the year. It shall be a perpetual statute throughout your generations; you shall celebrate it in the seventh month. You shall live in booths for seven days; all the native-born in Israel shall live in booths, so that your generations may know that I had the sons of Israel live in

*booths when I brought them out from the land of Egypt. I am the* LORD *your God.'"*

This section of scripture gives us the basic requirements of the feast. The week-long celebration began and ended with a Sabbath just as the other longer feasts have done. The people would bring their gifts, including their tithes (*Deuteronomy 14:22-26*) to Jerusalem (*Deuteronomy 16:13-15*) and offer sacrifices. The time was a great feast where rich and poor alike shared their resources and celebrated the end of the growing season. During this time, they were to live in temporary shelters explaining the names Feast of Booths and Feast of Tabernacles (These are two of the three names for this feast, the final being the Feast of Ingathering). The days in between the Sabbaths were also days of great sacrifice as described in *Numbers 29:12-38*. Each day saw a communal sacrifice of two rams and fourteen lambs, but also bulls, starting with 13 of them on the first day, then reducing the amount sacrificed to seven bulls on the seventh day. The eighth day was a Sabbath after which the people made the return trip home.

Like other feasts, God did not just want the Israelites to have a celebration like the pagans around them so this feast was dedicated to the remembrance of the wilderness wanderings when the people had lived in temporary shelters in the wilderness. This is also a remarkable day in the Christian life: The day of Pentecost.

## ISRAEL'S OTHER SACRED DAYS

Four other days are considered sacred in the Israelite community but the people were not specifically commanded to gather at the place where God had chosen. Two of these days, The Feast of Trumpets and The Day of Atonement were described in the Levitical Law. Purin was established after the Jewish protection in the time of Ester, and The Feast of Dedication was established during the period of prophetic silence but is recorded in the Apocryphal Maccabees books. We will consider a small study of each of these events because they were all established before the time of Christ.

The Feast of Trumpets commemorated the beginning of the Sabbath month. The land was shedding its final produce for the year and would be at rest until the sowing of the barley. This is set as the first day of the seventh month of the Jewish calendar and was a Sabbath but the people were commanded to offer an additional sacrifice to what was already required. The event was the beginning of the month the people celebrated the Day of Atonement and The Feast of Booths. *Numbers 29:1-6* describes the event:

> *'Now in the seventh month, on the first day of the month, you shall also have a holy convocation; you shall do no laborious work. It will be to you a day for blowing trumpets. You shall offer a burnt offering as a soothing aroma to the LORD: one bull, one ram, and seven male lambs one year old without defect; also their grain offering, fine flour mixed with oil: three-tenths of an ephah (6.3 quarts) for the bull, two-tenths for the ram (2.18 quarts), and one-tenth (1.09 quarts) for each of the seven lambs. Offer one male goat for a sin offering, to make atonement for you, besides the burnt offering of the new moon and its grain offering, and the continual burnt offering and its grain offering, and their drink offerings, according to their ordinance, for a soothing aroma, an offering by fire to the LORD.*

The Day of Atonement is a solemn day to be humbled before the Lord and to confess sins. This was a day for the people to offer a sacrifice for their sins, and also for the high priest to offer a sacrifice for the sins that were not confessed. The complete priestly practice is described in *Leviticus 16:2-34*. The command to the people is recounted by Moses as he detailed the other holy days and feasts:

> *On exactly the tenth day of this seventh month is the day of atonement; it shall be a holy convocation for you, and you shall humble your souls*

*and present an offering by fire to the LORD. You shall not do any work on this same day, for it is a day of atonement, to make atonement on your behalf before the LORD your God. If there is any person who will not humble himself on this same day, he shall be cut off from his people. As for any person who does any work on this same day, that person I will destroy from among his people. You shall do no work at all. It is to be a perpetual statute throughout your generations in all your dwelling places. It is to be a sabbath of complete rest to you, and you shall humble your souls; on the ninth of the month at evening, from evening until evening you shall keep your sabbath (Leviticus 23:27-32).*

Purim was not described by Moses or handed down from God like the other days we have examined, but the purpose and establishment are described in Esther. Haman wanted to destroy the Jews because Mordecai would not bow down to him as he passed on the streets (*Esther 3:1-6*). Haman used his influence with the king to establish a day when the Jews could be destroyed by the people in the kingdom. When the plan was discovered, Mordecai convinced Esther to make the plot known to the king. Since the law of the king could never be overturned, a new law was established for the same day allowing the Jews to defend themselves. On that day they were vindicated and that became a day of celebration.

The Feast of Dedication was a Jewish feast spanning several days and is now the holiday of Hanukkah. This was to commemorate the liberation of Jerusalem during the days of Maccabee. We include this as a holiday because it was celebrated in the time of Christ (*John 10:22*).

# General Bibliography

The Book of Days: A Miscellany of Popular Antiquities, 1836, R. Chambers

Brands Popular Antiquities for Great Britain, 1905, W Carew Hazlitt

The Every Day Book, 1825, William Hone

The History of the Christian Church, 1910, Philip Schaff

Institutes of the Christian Religion, 1534 (Hendrickson 2008 edition), John Calvin

National Retail Federation

*Specific references are listed throughout the text as footnotes

# Scripture Index

## New Testament

1 Corinthians 10............26
1 Corinthians 11............24
1 Corinthians 524, 99, 171
1 Corinthians 6............127
1 Corinthians 7..........73p.
1 Corinthians 8.........125p.
1 Corinthians 9.............23
1 Peter 4.....................56
1 Thessalonians 5.....146, 166
1 Timothy 6..................38
2 Corinthians 11............56
2 Corinthians 9...........103
2 Peter 1...............59, 94
2 Timothy 1.................94
2 Timothy 3...........26, 59
2 Timothy 4...............165
Acts 12.......................22
Acts 15..............23, 126p.
Acts 17.....................151
Acts 20.....................99p.
Acts 8........................31
Colossians 2.................23

Ephesians 1................146
Ephesians 2..................61
Ephesians 4. .26, 123, 127
Ephesians 5.................78
Galatians 4..................24
Galatians 5.........127, 166
Hebrews 11..................56
Hebrews 12..................77
Hebrews 13..................40
James 5.......................41
John 10......................179
John 15.......................77
John 5........................22
John 7........................22
Luke 12.......................37
Luke 22.......................58
Luke 6........................38
Mark 11......................110
Mark 14.......................24
Mark 4........................36
Matthew 16..........32, 171
Matthew 19..................39
Matthew 25..................61
Matthew 5..........56, 78p.

Matthew 6............41, 122
Philippians 2................57
Philippians 4..38, 40, 145
Revelation 2................75
Romans 10...........25, 125
Romans 12..................123
Romans 14..................23
Romans 3.....................25
Romans 5.....................25

**Old Testament.....................**
1 Chronicles 23.............19
1 Samuel 20.................19
2 Chronicles 29.............19
2 Chronicles 30.............19
2 Chronicles 35............20
2 Chronicles 36............20
2 Chronicles 6.......15, 169
2 Kings 22....................19
2 Samuel 11..................31
2 Samuel 23.................30
2 Samuel 24.................18
Deuteronomy 14.........177
Deuteronomy 16..15, 169,
177
Deuteronomy 17............16
Deuteronomy 28...16, 59,
176
Deuteronomy 31.........144

Deuteronomy 8............39
Ecclesiastes 3..............163
Ecclesiastes 5............36p.
Esther 3......................179
Esther 9........................55
Exodus 12......54, 58, 92,
170pp.
Exodus 20....................29
Ezra 3...........................21
Jeremiah 25.................20
Jeremiah 29.................20
Joshua 24....................145
Joshua 6.......................30
Joshua 7.......................30
Leviticus 12............53, 68
Leviticus 16................178
Leviticus 23.......54, 100,
173p., 176, 179
Micah 2.........................32
Nehemiah 8.................21
Numbers 29.............177p.
Proverbs 11...................43
Proverbs 17..................42
Proverbs 21.....32, 35, 43
Proverbs 22..................42
Proverbs 30.................40
Proverbs 5....................73
Proverbs 6...................43

# About the Authors

**Thomas Murosky** has a background in the Biological Sciences earning his Bachelors in Biochemistry and Doctorate in Molecular Toxicology. He has taught at Bucknell University and Western Wyoming Community College. While as a student and professor, Tom worked in several capacities as a children's and youth worker having served the local CEF board, as a counselor for Christian camps, Awana programs, and other youth outreach including a decade of work in Big Brothers, Big Sisters of America.

He stepped aside from teaching and academics to work as a technology consultant to focus more time on writing, blogging, and video production in the area of Christian teaching with a focus on discipleship and sanctification.

You can find more information and other books Thomas has authored at www.ourwalkinchrist.com.

**Tyler Gayan** works on a variety of media projects including writing, poetry, and music production. As of co-writing Happy Hellidays, he is a recent high school graduate.

Aside from his media work he enjoys spending time with his family and with animals. He has been a lifelong church attendee, but came to a true knowledge of faith after wrestling with, and overcoming, a battle with sin. It was God who helped him to see Christ.

# Other Books by Thomas Murosky

## I AM not amused

ISBN:

978-1-7325696-2-1 (s)

978-1-7325696-3-8 (e)

Does your entertainment honor God?

## Testing and Temptations

ISBN:

978-1-7325696-0-7 (s)

978-1-7325696-1-4 (e)

Do you know what it takes to live like Jesus?

## Josiah's Sanctification

ISBN:

978-1-732569645 (s)

978-1-7325696-5-2 (e)

What can you learn about Sanctification from an ancient king?

Made in the USA
Middletown, DE
18 October 2020